CALMING STREAMS
ENCOURAGING MESSAGES

To: Sis. Frankie

CALMING STREAMS
ENCOURAGING MESSAGES

Prayer with Each Message

To Sis. Frankie

MOLETHA FOWLER-THOMPSON

XULON PRESS

Xulon Press
2301 Lucien Way #415
Maitland, FL 32751
407.339.4217
www.xulonpress.com

Paperback ISBN-13: 978-1-66282-896-6
Hard Cover ISBN-13: 978-1-66282-897-3
Ebook ISBN-13: 978-1-66282-898-0

TABLE OF CONTENTS

Introduction

*For I will pour water on the thirsty land, and streams on the
dry ground; I will pour out my Spirit on your offspring, and
my blessing on your descendants.*

—Isaiah 44:3 (NIV)

Calming streams never stop flowing into the lives of those who thirst for wisdom, knowledge, and an understanding of God's Word. He will lead you to calming streams, during times of despair. We obtain rest when we know and believe the promises of God.

Each day you read *Calming Streams,* I hope you gain an increased prayer life and increased faith. I hope you are strengthened with every message and give praise to God for all of His goodness. You will read messages that will remind you of God's healing power.

Included in the book is a chapter on self-care: how to choose healthy foods, begin an exercise program, and grow a spiritual garden, complete with examples of healthy foods and starter exercises. There is also a prayer after every message. Each prayer is written in faith, believing that God knows what you need in every area of your life. Through faith, He will bless and meet the needs of each person reading *Calming Streams.*

Moletha Fowler-Thompson

PRAYER

Dear Heavenly Father, I pray You will open the spiritual eyes of each one reading *Calming Streams*. Through each message, I pray for minds to be touched, understanding and guidance to be given, and growth in trusting You. I pray these messages will minister to the whole person emotionally, spiritually, and physically. These blessings I pray for, in the mighty name of Jesus. Amen.

LISTEN FOR GOD'S VOICE

So then faith comet by hearing, and hearing by the word of God.
—Romans 10:14 (KJV)

L istening to the Word of God provides encouragement, wisdom, knowledge, and faith. The apostle Paul encouraged all believers to engage in listening and prayer.

Rejoicing in hope; patient in tribulation; continuing instant in prayer

—Romans 12:12 (KJV)

Choose a quiet place for your prayer meetings with God, during a calm time of your day. You don't have to kneel, but closing your eyes will assist you in mentally connecting with God. God wants to hear your heart's desires, and He wants you to hear His answers to your prayers.

Elijah was a prophet of God. In 1 Kings 19:2–3, when Jezebel threatened to kill him, he ran for his life. When Elijah reached Horeb, the mountain of God, he spent the night in a cave. Later, the word of the Lord came to him and asked, "What are you doing here, Elijah?" (1 Kings 19:9, NKJV). After Elijah gave his explanation, in verse 11, the Lord told him to "Go out and stand on the mountain in the presence of the Lord, for the Lord is about to pass by."

And God's responded, "And a great and strong wind tore into the mountains and broke the rocks in pieces before the LORD, *but* the LORD *was* not in the wind; and after the wind an earthquake, *but* the LORD *was* not in the earthquake; and after the earthquake a fire, *but* the LORD *was* not in the fire; and after the fire a still small voice. (1 Kings 19:11–12, NKJV).

The lesson here is to listen for and recognize God's calm, quiet voice. He may speak to you when you're praying, while you're worshiping, or while you're reading His Word.

PRAYER

Dear Heavenly Father, thank You for hearing the prayers of each reader. Thank You for hearing the very desires of their hearts. Thank You for giving them the patience to wait for their prayers to be answered. Thank You for teaching them through Your Word. I praise You for their todays, tomorrows, and every day the readers have an opportunity to communicate with You. I pray You will bless and keep each reader, make Your face to shine upon them, be gracious, lift Your countenance upon them, and give them peace. I ask these blessings, in the name of Jesus. Amen.

YOUR THOUGHTS AND PRAYER REQUEST

_____

_____

_____

_____

_____

_____

_____

_____

_____

_____

_____

_____

_____

_____

_____

_____

_____

Be Confident

Now this is the confidence that we have in Him, that if we ask anything according to His will, He hears us.

—1 John 5:14 (NKJV)

Have confidence and compassion in prayer as you send your requests to God. He hears the prayers of those who communicate with Him. Your prayer does not have to be long; it doesn't have to be loud; it doesn't have to contain eloquent words. Be confident that God hears the content of your prayers, no matter how you're saying them. David said, "Delight yourselves also in the Lord and he shall give you the desires of your heart" (Ps. 37:4, KJV).

When you're praying for a need, tell God what it is, and be specific. Should you need healing, say what the healing need is and where you need it. If you have a financial need, say the need and ask the Lord to bless you. Encourage yourself even more by reading scriptures that speak to your specific need.

Be confident in knowing that Jesus will meet you where you are: in the courthouse, in the hospital, or on your job. If you're a single mother living on a limited income, God will meet you. If you're in the kitchen, cooking with limited meal planning, Jesus will meet you. In every situation of your life, Jesus will meet you.

The first-person Jesus met after He rose out of the grave was Mary Magdalene. She didn't know the person she was speaking with was Jesus, but He inquired, "Why are you weeping?" Mary looked at this person and asked if He knew where Jesus was taken. After Jesus said her name, Mary knew it was He (John 20:14–16, NKJV).

This passage of scripture lets us know that God met Mary Magdalene when she least expected Him. God will meet you wherever you are, as well.

PRAYER

Dear Heavenly Father, I pray You will make each person reading today's message confident in knowing that You hear their prayers, regardless of where they may be. I pray that they know You are aware of all the desires of their hearts and that You see and hear their needs. I speak blessings into their lives, in the mighty name of Jesus. Amen.

YOUR THOUGHTS AND PRAYER REQUEST

_____

_____

_____

_____

_____

_____

_____

_____

_____

_____

_____

_____

_____

_____

_____

_____

FOLLOW GOD'S INSTRUCTIONS

I will instruct you and teach you in the way you should go; I will guide you with My eye.

—Psalm 32:8 (NKJV)

I'm excited to encourage each reader to follow God's instructions for their lives. It's socially acceptable for friends and family to give instructions to the best of their knowledge. However, God is the one who knows the deepest secrets and desires of your heart, and only He knows your future.

Imagine what would have happened to Moses if his mother, Jochebed, had not followed the instructions God was putting in her heart. She knew about Pharaoh's order to kill every Hebrew boy at birth. After Jochebed nursed Moses for three months, she waterproofed a basket and put it among the reeds of the Nile River. Moses grew up in the rich environment of Pharoah's daughter. Staying true to his purpose, Moses led the Israelites out of bondage.

Samuel, on the other hand, heard God's instructions but misinterpreted them. God sent him to anoint the next king of Israel. Samuel saw Jesse's son, Eliab, and assumed he was the one he was supposed to anoint, but he wasn't.

In fact, Jesse introduced seven of his sons to Samuel, but none of the seven were to be anointed.

Then, in 1 Samuel 16:11, Jesse had one more son but thought he could not possibly be the one Samuel was to anoint because of his appearance. So, Samuel left him in the field to tend the sheep. God had already told him, in 1 Samuel 13:14, that He was looking for the one person after His own heart to rule over His people, but Samuel had not perceived God's earlier instructions to him.

In 1 Samuel 16:13, Samuel anointed David, the one God had chosen to be king over Israel, in the presence of all his brothers. It didn't matter that he was a sheep herder; it was his heart that mattered to God. Those of you reading this message, learn from Samuel. Choose to listen to God's instruction instead of your own.

PRAYER

Thank You, Jesus, for knowing the heart of each reader and for not judging by the outer appearance. I pray You will make each reader authentically themselves. I pray that when each one hears from You, they will have a desire to understand and follow Your instructions. I ask for these blessings, in the name of Jesus. Amen.

YOUR THOUGHTS AND PRAYER REQUEST

_____

_____

_____

_____

_____

_____

_____

_____

_____

_____

_____

_____

_____

_____

_____

_____

_____

_____

LET GO OF WORRY

Casting all your cares upon Him, for He cares for you.

—1 Peter 5:7 (NKJV)

I want to encourage all who are reading today's message to let go of your worries and give them to Jesus. Give Him your fears, disappointments, depression, anger, loss, and anxiety. Handing all your problems to Jesus will result in securing peace and calmness in your life.

Take one problem at a time and put it at Jesus's feet. When you do, say the name of that problem, and listen to what you're saying. Say, for example, "Dear Jesus, I've been worrying about my lack of income. But I trust You. I have faith that my income is increasing."

By letting go of that one worry, you're stepping off that endless merry-go-round the devil wants to keep you on. He wants you to continue to go round and round with no results. But through faith and consistent prayer, you're moving forward as you let God take care of every problem in your life.

Now that you're letting go of each problem one at a time and giving it to Jesus, you're going to experience God's peace that passes all understanding. Peace is the opposite of worry. Day by day, keep your thoughts in a right standing with God's Word.

It's time to stop basking in self-pity. Let go of everything you've been worrying about, cast all your cares upon Jesus, and then get up and move forward. Do what the four leprous men in 2 Kings 7:3–8 did. Because of their illness, they couldn't go into the city. They had to sit outside at the gate and worry about their fate. One day, they made a decision to either sit and die or get up. Their determination to march into the Syrians' camp prompted God's power.

God made the lepers' footsteps sound like an army of chariots and horses. That noise caused fear in the minds of the Syrians, and they rushed out of their tents. All four lepers went into the camp and feasted on the food and drink the Syrians left behind and walked away with their silver, gold, and raiment. All four men stopped thinking and speaking worry, grabbed hold of faith, spoke it, and moved forward.

PRAYER

Dear Savior, I ask that You give strength to each reader. Help them hand over to You their worries and fears. I pray You will teach each one how to lay aside every weight and move forward with a light heart, with faith. I ask for each one to be steadfast in prayer and trust in You. I ask that these significant blessings be answered, in the name of Jesus. Amen.

YOUR THOUGHTS AND PRAYER REQUEST

_____

_____

_____

_____

_____

_____

_____

_____

_____

_____

_____

_____

_____

_____

_____

_____

Call on Jesus

So Jesus said to them, Because of your unbelief; for assuredly,
I say to you, if you have faith as a mustard seed, you will say
to this mountain, Move from here to there,' and it will move;
and nothing will be impossible for you.

—Matthew 17:20 (NKJV)

In today's message, I want to encourage you to call on Jesus in every situation of your life. If you feel like crying, do so with faith. If you have a difficult day, stand firm in prayer and give God praise.

During difficult times, it's okay to weep. God will still hear your prayers. Blind Bartimaeus was sitting by the road, begging, when he heard those around him say Jesus was nearby. After hearing this, faith and desperation took over, and he immediately and loudly cried out to Jesus and asked Him for mercy.

Many who were around blind Bartimaeus told him to be quiet, but he cried out more. Jesus heard his cry and called for blind Bartimaeus to come to Him. Then He asked him, "What do you want Me to do for you?" (Mark 10:51, NKJV).

Blind Bartimaeus told Jesus he wanted to receive his sight. After hearing his request, Jesus told him, "Go your way; your faith has made you well" (Mark 10:52, NKJV).

If you need something from Jesus, cry out to Him and tell Him what you want Him to do for you. When you do, believe and trust Him to fulfill every request. Faith is of the essence in every call. God hears a prayer that's presented even with faith the size of a mustard seed. A mustard seed is the smallest of seeds, but it can grow into a bush thirty feet tall and wide. Jesus wants you to know that just a little bit of faith will produce a great change in your life.

In Matthew 17:20, the word *mountain* symbolizes any area of your life that needs to be moved. If it's sickness, believe the sickness is gone. If it's low self-esteem, believe it's gone. If it's envy, believe it's gone. If it's fear or anger, believe it's gone. If it's jealousy, believe it's gone. Whatever the mountain is, ask God to move it out of your way, and believe that He will.

PRAYER

Dear Heavenly Father, thank You for hearing the call of each person reading today's message. I praise You for each of my readers, for their tomorrows, and for every moment they call out to You. Thank You for hearing the very desires of their hearts. Lord, I pray You will teach them every spiritual message through Your Word and give them patience to wait for you to answer their prayers. I pray You will bless and keep each one and make Your face to shine upon them. Be gracious to each one, lift Your countenance unto them, and give them peace. I ask for these blessings, in the name of Jesus. Amen.

Your Thoughts and Prayer Request

_____

_____

_____

_____

_____

_____

_____

_____

_____

_____

_____

_____

_____

_____

_____

_____

PRAYER WITH PRAISE

I will bless the LORD at all times; His praise shall continually be in my mouth.

—Psalm 34:1 (NKJV)

Today's message is written to encourage readers to praise God for what He has done for them and what He is going to do. When you give Him praise, God will give you strength to pray through every situation and peace that goes beyond your understanding. "He gives power to the weak, And to *those who have* no might He increases strength" (Isa. 40:20, NKJV).

I want to inspire each of you to praise God because He is your Lord and Savior. Praise Him for His healing power. Praise Him for keeping you safe. Praise Him for providing. Praise Him for increased faith. Praise Him for being your protector. Praise Him for giving you a mind to do good works. Praise Him for your future blessings.

Prayer plus praise equals blessings. Know that God will go before you and make the crooked paths straight. There's so much you can't see with your natural eyes. You can't see your future or the difficult days that may be ahead of you, so you can't plan a way to avoid or escape these times ahead. Only God knows your future, so keep praising and praying to Him.

According to Isaiah 42:16, God wants you to know He will lead you through the areas of your life that you know nothing about. He will make the darkness light before you, and He will supply your needs in abundance. Philippians tells you to "Be anxious for nothing, but in everything by prayer and supplication, with thanksgiving, let your requests be made known to God; and the peace of God, which surpasses all understanding, will guard your hearts and minds through Christ Jesus" (Phil. 4:6–7, NKJV).

PRAYER

I praise You, Jesus, for all You have done for those who are reading today's message. I lift my hands to heaven and give You praise. I lift my voice in admiration of Your goodness, faithfulness, and kindness toward each one. I give You all the praise, acknowledgment, and appreciation for what You are doing and for what You will be doing. I pray You will go before each person reading and make their crooked paths straight. I ask for these blessings, in the mighty name of Jesus. Amen.

YOUR THOUGHTS AND PRAYER REQUEST

_____

_____

_____

_____

_____

_____

_____

_____

_____

_____

_____

_____

_____

_____

_____

Trust God

Trust in the LORD with all your heart, And lean not on your own understanding; In all your ways acknowledge Him, And He shall direct your paths.

—Proverbs 3:5–6 (NKJV)

Today's message is to motivate each reader to communicate with God, through prayer, in all things. It doesn't matter what your eyes see. Accept your knowledge of God and your experience of His great power. Accept what your heart knows and believes.

Trust God, for He is a promise keeper. During a three-year drought, God promised the prophet Elijah that He would send rain to Israel, but He didn't tell Elijah when this would happen. Looking with his natural eyes, he couldn't see the promise, but he kept trusting God. Holding on to that trust, Elijah started making his request known to God in prayer. At the end of each prayer, Elijah instructed his servant to go and look for signs of rain. The servant looked, but when he returned, he reported that he hadn't seen any signs of rain.

Each time God sent his servant to go look for signs of God's promise, he was trusting God. When he sent his servant out for the seventh time, the servant returned and told Elijah he saw a small cloud in the sky about the size of a man's hand. At this moment, Elijah's trust in God was strengthened. After three years without rain in Israel, God's promise was fulfilled.

Judges 4:14–15 is written about a courageous leader named Deborah. She trusted God, and He was present in her life and in her leadership over the people of Israel. No matter the battle or situation, Deborah believed the victory was already in her favor because she had put her trust in God.

I have a special request for all readers: do not be concerned about how long it takes to receive an answer to your prayers. Hold on to your heart's desire and keep praying for what you have asked God to do in your life, and trust Him that He will answer in His time.

PRAYER

Heavenly Father, my prayer today is that You will help each reader see with their spiritual eyes, trusting in You, with faith, that You are meeting all their needs. Touch the spiritual eyes of each one so they will see signs of their prayers being answered and their needs being met. Let them see even the smallest evidence to strengthen their faith and wait for You to do what may seem impossible in their lives. I pray for these blessings, in the powerful name of Jesus. Amen.

YOUR THOUGHTS AND PRAYER REQUEST

_____

_____

_____

_____

_____

_____

_____

_____

_____

_____

_____

_____

_____

_____

_____

_____

ABUNDANT LIFE

> *I have come that they may have life, and that they may have*
> *it more abundantly.*
>
> —John 10:10 (NKJV)

In presenting today's message, I hope everyone will welcome the spiritual meaning of "abundant life." Some may think the abundant life refers to having a lot of money. Others may think it means acquiring every material item the world has to offer. This is because the first part of John 10:10 often gets ignored.

With encouragement as well as hope for a better understanding, I present the entire verse. "The thief does not come except to steal, and to kill, and to destroy. I have come that they may have life, and that they may have *it* more abundantly" (John 10:10, NKJV).

The thief, the devil, is the one who misleads those who believe in Jesus and His Word. There may be times when a teaching of Scripture will be misleading. It may be sincere, but it lacks understanding of God's Word. I desire that not one person is led away from trusting, believing, and understanding the Word of God. A most essential part of having an abundant life is believing and confessing, "For God so loved the world that He gave His only begotten Son, that whoever believes in Him should not perish but have everlasting life" (John 3:16, NKJV).

It's not a sin to have nice earthly possessions. Nevertheless, God does want believers to know that John 10:10 is about having a more abundant spiritual life through Him.

A believer who has very little in their bank account, who has a limited income, who has little to eat, who has little clothing, who has one pair of shoes, or who has no transportation can have an abundant spiritual life. It's not defined by what a believer possesses.

I very much enjoy the television ministry of Joseph Prince. He's the evangelist and senior pastor of New Creation Church, based in Singapore. I'd like to share with all my readers some of his message about the abundant life:

"When you feed on Jesus, the most well-loved psalm in the Bible, Psalm 23, paints a beautiful picture of our good shepherd, Jesus, caring for His beloved flock. He feeds, protects, and leads us to rest so that we lack no good thing. You can experience the abundant life that Jesus has for you when you allow Him to shepherd and feed you. When you focus on Him and feed on His love for you and on His living words, you will find rest for your souls, victory over the most trying circumstances, and an abundance of every good thing! The abundant life refers to life in its abounding fullness of joy and strength for spirit, soul, and body."

PRAYER

Dear Heavenly Father, today I want to thank You for all who believe, everywhere, from all walks of life and in every culture. I pray You will give each one reading today's message a clear mind when reading Your Word. I pray for understanding of Your love for all, no matter the height, the weight, the skin color, or the economic status. I am so grateful that Your love is everlasting from generation to generation. I pray for the abundant life for each reader. I pray You will give fullness of joy and strength. I ask for these blessings to be passed from generation to generation, in the mighty name of Jesus. Amen.

Your Thoughts and Prayer Request

_____

_____

_____

_____

_____

_____

_____

_____

_____

_____

_____

_____

_____

_____

_____

_____

THE SHEPHERD'S LOVE FOR HIS SHEEP

My sheep hear my voice, and I know them, and they follow me.
—John 10:27 (KJV)

Today's message is to emphasize the love Jesus has for all. Jesus has an endless love for those who believe and trust in Him. He lovingly refers to those people as His sheep. "For he is our God; and we are the people of his pasture, and the sheep of his hand" (Ps. 95:7, KJV).

In the natural, sheep follow their shepherd and receive comfort when they hear his voice. Likewise, those who believe in Jesus are to follow Him; the sheep who hear His voice are led to safety. The Shepherd wants His sheep to know, "I will never leave you nor forsake you" (Heb. 13:5, NKJV). David said, "He is my refuge and my fortress; My God, in Him I will trust" (Ps. 91:2, NKJV). There is safety when we abide in the presence of God.

God's sheep are to trust His Word, not feelings or circumstances. Make certain you reinforce God's Word by your faith, even when emotions tempt you to believe something different than what the Shepherd says. When changes occur in your life, know that "Jesus Christ is the same yesterday, today, and forever" (Heb. 13:8, NKJV).

There have been many great lieutenants in the military and powerful presidents. However, none have been able to match or surpass the power of the Shepherd. His eyes are everywhere in the world, and His ears are open to every prayer, twenty-four hours a day, seven days a week. You don't have to schedule an appointment with Him, and He will never close His door to you.

PRAYER

Dear Heavenly Father, I pray You will be the Shepherd for those who are reading today's message so that they will not want. I pray they will lie down in green pastures and that You will lead them beside still waters. I pray You will restore their souls and lead them in the paths of righteousness for Your name's sake. When each one walks through the valley of the shadow of death, let them know it is only a shadow. I pray each one reading will not fear the devil's evil attachments on their life. I pray You will be with them and give comfort through every trial, every tribulation, and every disappointment. I pray You will prepare a table for each reader in the presence of their enemies. Anoint their heads with oil, and let their blessings go over and above what they may think or imagine. I pray for and believe You will cause goodness and mercy to follow each one, all the days of their life, and for them to dwell in Your Heavenly home forever. I ask for these blessings, in the name of Jesus. Amen.

YOUR THOUGHTS AND PRAYER REQUEST

_____

_____

_____

_____

_____

_____

_____

_____

_____

_____

_____

_____

_____

_____

_____

_____

MAKE WISE DECISIONS

Wisdom is the principal thing; Therefore get wisdom. And in all your getting, get understanding.

—Proverbs 4:7 (NKJV)

Today's message is to encourage all readers to ask God for a discerning heart to make better decisions. This is what Solomon asked God for in the book of Proverbs so he could govern his people and distinguish between right and wrong.

God was pleased with Solomon's request and told him, "Because you have asked this thing, and have not asked long life for yourself, nor have asked riches for yourself, nor have asked the life of your enemies, but have asked for yourself understanding to discern justice, behold, I have done according to your words..." (1 Kings 3:11–12, NKJV). God was so content with Solomon's request that He gave him what he did not ask for: wealth, honor, and a long life.

Wisdom is an important attribute that will help you make better decisions throughout your life. It will assist you in using your knowledge every day. Solomon had a lot of knowledge, but he needed wisdom to know how to use the knowledge God had already given him. In chapter 1 of James, we learn that if you need wisdom, you simply need to ask God. And when you ask, do it with faith, and don't doubt. James compares doubting to the waves of the sea. God does not want anyone who believes in Him to be "driven and tossed by the wind" (James 1:6, NKJV).

I don't want those reading today's message to think I'm minimizing knowledge and understanding, because they are powerful. This combination will definitely assist you in making better decisions. But accumulated knowledge and experience about many things become more powerful when linked with wisdom. Understanding encompasses both wisdom and knowledge. Believers who have all three will have the ability to use good judgment and make wise choices in all areas of life.

Prayer

Dear Heavenly Father, I pray You will help those who are reading today's message to use wisdom and knowledge in every choice they make. I pray each reader will know how to apply their wisdom and knowledge with an understanding in every choice and every decision. I pray they will be encouraged and inspired when they read Your Word. These blessings I ask You for in the mighty name of Jesus. Amen.

Your Thoughts and Prayer Request

_____

_____

_____

_____

_____

_____

_____

_____

_____

_____

_____

_____

_____

_____

_____

_____

_____

A Shining Light

You are the light of the world. A city that is set on a hill cannot be hidden. Nor do they light a lamp and put it under a basket, but on a lampstand, and it gives light to all who are in the house. Let your light so shine before men, that they may see your good works and glorify your Father in heaven.

—Matthew 5:14–16 (NKJV)

Those who love Jesus and obey His Word are encouraged to live a life that's pleasing in the sight of our Lord and Savior. When you do, others will notice your good works, accept your words of comfort, and hear you when you speak about God's Word. Let your character be a radiant light that attracts others so they will hear you when you talk about the love and goodness of Jesus. You can lead others into a more fulfilling life. Their impossible will become possible once they accept Jesus into their lives.

This light does not shine suddenly. It grows over time, and due to your active prayer life, your faith in God's Word, and your adherence to its teachings, your light will shine bright. You are following the greatest light the world has ever known: Jesus, the light of the world. Jesus said, "I am the light of the world. He who follows Me shall not walk in darkness, but have the light of life" (John 8:12, NKJV).

My hope is that when you're surrounded by darkness and unbelievers, you can be the light. Let those who don't believe in Jesus notice your character. As one of Jesus's followers, your character will tell others who you are and will hold true to your testimony.

PRAYER

Dear Heavenly Father, I pray You will bless each one reading today's message. I pray each of them will have a desire to walk according to Your Word and to be a shining light so others will hear and accept You as their personal Savior. I ask for each reader to be an example of Your grace and to believe the steps of a righteous person are ordered by the Lord. I pray for each one to trust and be a witness for You, through their character. I ask for these blessings, in the name of Jesus. Amen.

YOUR THOUGHTS AND PRAYER REQUEST

_____

_____

_____

_____

_____

_____

_____

_____

_____

_____

_____

_____

_____

_____

_____

_____

God's Favor

So it was, when the king saw Queen Esther standing in the court, that she found favor in his sight, and the king held out to Esther the golden scepter that was in his hand...

—Esther 5:2 (NKJV)

Today's message is to prompt those reading to see God's favor in their lives, because God's favor means approval. I'm not talking about favoritism; God does not show partiality. He loves everyone the same. But those who don't love God shouldn't expect to receive favor from Him. Along with loving God and obtaining His favor is caring for others through praying for and fasting for one another, giving food and water to the hungry, and extending a helping hand to those in need.

Ruth 2:11–12 shows Ruth obtaining God's favor because of her faithfulness to her mother-in-law, Naomi. As a result of being noticed for the things she had done, she received special treatment and protection, which added up to be more than enough.

The book of Ruth clearly shows God being fair, just, and faithful to those who believe and trust in Him. Ruth showed her faithfulness to Naomi, Boaz was faithful to Ruth, and all of them showed faithfulness to God. God's favor showed in His many blessings to them.

Of all the kings of Judah, Hezekiah was the most obedient to God. As a result, he found favor in His eyes. In acknowledgment, God answered Hezekiah's prayer and added fifteen years to his life. "In those days Hezekiah was sick and near death. And Isaiah the prophet, the son of Amoz, went to him and said to him, Thus says the LORD: 'Set your house in order, for you shall die, and not live" (2 Kings 20:1, NKJV).

After Hezekiah heard this, he turned his face toward the wall, and prayed to the LORD, saying, "Remember now, O LORD, I pray, how I have walked before You in truth and with a loyal heart, and have done *what was good* in Your sight. And Hezekiah wept bitterly" (2 Kings 20:2–3, NKJV).

Hezekiah's honest and sincere prayer request moved God. So He told Isaiah to go back and "tell Hezekiah the leader of My people, 'Thus says the LORD, the God of David your father: "I have heard your prayer, I have seen your tears; surely I will heal you. On the third day you shall go up to the house of the LORD'" (2 Kings 20:5, NKJV).

I hope today's message has encouraged each reader in knowing they, too, can acquire God's favor.

PRAYER

Thank You, Jesus, for awakening each reader's understanding about Your favor. I pray You will encourage each one to become stronger in their faithfulness toward You and others. I pray for guidance in receiving Your favor and Your faithfulness. I praise You and glorify You, Lord, for all Your goodness toward each reader. I ask for these blessings, in the name of Jesus. Amen.

YOUR THOUGHTS AND PRAYER REQUEST

_____

_____

_____

_____

_____

_____

_____

_____

_____

_____

_____

_____

_____

_____

_____

_____

_____

BATTLES IN LIFE

And when the servant of the man of God arose early and went out, there was an army, surrounding the city with horses and chariots. And his servant said to him, "Alas, my master! What shall we do?" So he answered, "Do not fear, for those who are with us are more than those who are with them." And Elisha prayed, and said, "LORD, I pray, open his eyes that he may see." Then the LORD opened the eyes of the young man, and he saw. And behold, the mountain was full of horses and chariots of fire all around Elisha. So when the Syrians came down to him, Elisha prayed to the LORD, and said, "Strike this people, I pray, with blindness." And He struck them with blindness according to the word of Elisha.

—2 Kings 6:15–18 (NKJV)

There may be times in your life when you will have to battle depression, sickness, anxiety, a broken heart, pain, and weakness. Don't go into battle before taking hold of your spiritual weapons. Always take hold of prayer, which is simply communicating with God. "When you fast, do not look somber as the hypocrites do, for they disfigure their faces to show others they are fasting. Truly I tell you, they have received their reward in full" (Phil. 4:6, NKJV).

When facing life's battles, prepare for fasting with faith. In the New Testament, fasting is recommended as a way to grow closer to God. It's a personal discipline. "When you fast, do not look somber as the hypocrites do, for they disfigure their faces to show others they are fasting. Truly I tell you, they have their reward in full. But when you fast, put oil on your head and wash your face, so that it will not be obvious to others that you are fasting, but only to your father who is unseen; and your father, who sees what is done in secret, will reward you" (Matt. 6:16, NIV).

Battles require elevating faith, so you will need a firmly held belief in God's Word to elevate what you have been praying for. And when you ask, do not doubt. "But let him ask in faith, with no doubting, for he who doubts is like a wave of the sea driven and tossed by the wind" (James 1:6, NKJV).

It's also important not to stop praying when you're in a battle. Should you experience a mental battle, keep praying. If it's an emotional battle, keep praying. If it's a financial battle, keep praying. If you're battling against illness, keep praying. These are the times to let the devil know you are going to pray in every battle. Paise God in battles and read His Word. God knows the needs and He listen to your prayers.

The Lord heard Joshua and knew what to do for him. Joshua was a leader of the Israelites. While he was battling with his enemies, he asked God to cause the moon and the sun to stand still. "So the sun stood still, And the moon stopped, Till the people had revenge Upon their enemies" (Josh. 10:13, NKJV). Joshua knew the dark of night would confuse him and his army, so he wanted to leave no doubt who the enemy was. He also wanted to be sure that he and his army would not fight against each other. Therefore, with faith, Joshua asked God to stop the sun from going down.

Build on your faith and prayer life so you'll be ready for every battle. Don't allow the devil to feed you negative thoughts like "It's too hard." Instead, read the scriptures that pertain to your specific battle.

There was a time in my life when the Lord blessed me with desired employment. I lived in the southern part of a state, and this employment was in the northern part. Before I packed my belongings, I took my car to be serviced, and then I started traveling on a Saturday morning. The directions I copied led me up and around mountains. I thought, *Oh my God, I've never traveled this route,* and fear entered my mind. But I remembered to pray.

About an hour into my six-hour drive, rain started pouring down. This is when I realized the left windshield wiper wasn't working properly, and it became difficult to see. At this moment, I thought about when Joshua asked God to stop the sun. So, I prayed, "God, if You will just stop the rain, I will make it to my destination safely."

Immediately, the rain stopped. When I made it to my destination, I looked to my left and saw the address. Then I heard the soft, caring voice of the Lord telling me, "You asked me to stop the rain." After God spoke these words, it started to rain again, and it rained for days.

But Jesus looked at them and said, *With men it is impossible, but not with God; for with God all things are possible* (Mark 10:27, NKJV).

PRAYER

Thank You, Jesus, for giving each one reading today's message strength during their battles. I pray You will give each one a mind to pray and a strong faith to believe through every one. I pray each reader will hold on and trust You in every disappointment. Where there is discouragement, I pray for encouraging thoughts and words. I pray You will give strength to the ones who are battling through trials and tribulations and that You will bring them out of the battle with their hands lifted and their voices praising You. I pray for renewed confidence and trust in You, Lord. These blessings I ask for, in the mighty name of Jesus. Amen.

Your Thoughts and Prayer Request

_____

_____

_____

_____

_____

_____

_____

_____

_____

_____

_____

_____

_____

_____

_____

_____

_____

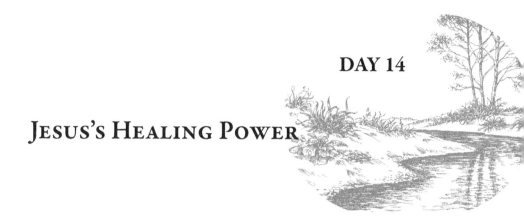

Jesus's Healing Power

Then Jesus went about all the cities and villages, teaching in their synagogues, preaching the gospel of the kingdom, and healing every sickness and every disease among the people.
—Matthew 9:35 (NKJV)

I call on prayer warriors with strong faith to pray for the sick and for those who have been told they have incurable illnesses, who are bound by alcohol or drug dependency, or who suffer from mental illness. Above all, I call on the healing power of Jesus. When Jesus walked this earth, He touched those who were sick or just told them they were healed.

When Jesus was preparing to heal a blind man, "He took the blind man by the hand and led him out of the town. And when He had spit on his eyes and put His hands on him, He asked him if he saw anything" (Mark 8:23, NKJV). This man told Jesus that people looked like trees. One more time, "He put *His* hands on his eyes again and made him look up. And he was restored and saw everyone clearly" (Mark 8:25, NKJV).

Another time, Jesus used mud to heal a blind man. He spit on the ground, made clay, and then anointed the man's eyes with it (John 9:6). Next Jesus told him to, "Go, wash in the pool of Siloam" (John 9:7, NKJV). After following Jesus' instructions, the blind man could see.

Jesus healed Jarius's daughter through touch and His spoken word. He took her hand and said, 'Talitha, cumi,' which is translated, 'Little girl, I say to you, arise'" (Mark 5:41, NKJV). Luke wrote about the ten men who had leprosy, which is an infection that affects the nerves, skin, eyes, and lining of the nose. The ten men loudly called out to Jesus and asked Him to have pity on them. So, Jesus told them to go show themselves to the priest. "As they went, they were cleansed" (Luke 17:14, NKJV). But even though all ten men were healed, only one man returned to praise Jesus and thank him. Jesus told the man, "Arise, go your way. Your faith has made you well" (Luke 17:19).

Every now and then, I quietly think of God's goodness and His miraculous healing power. These thoughts remind me of a song I listened to in the church I attended when I was a child. Sometimes I still softly sing this song because it blesses my soul and leads me to praise God. The lyrics are, "Oh, when I think about the goodness of Jesus and all that He has done for me, my soul cries out, Hallelujah, Hallelujah. I thank God for saving me."

The power of Jesus's healing touch and His love were again demonstrated when He went to the home of Simon Peter's mother-in-law. "And when Jesus was come into Peter's house, he saw his wife's mother laid, and sick of a fever. And he touched her hand, and the fever left her: and she arose, and ministered unto them" (Matt. 8:14–15, KJV).

I also need to talk about a woman who was so desperate to be healed that she touched the hem of the garment Jesus was wearing. She had given all her money to the physicians, hoping they would heal her, but after exhausting all her finances, she remembered hearing about the healing power of Jesus. One day, she saw people crowded around Him and started reasoning to herself, "If I could just touch the hem of His garment, I will be healed" (Matthew 9:21, NKJV). Pressing her way into the crowd, she finally touched the hem. Immediately, Jesus wanted to know who had touched Him. Even though there was a crowd of people around Jesus, touching Him, they must have lacked the faith to be healed, either physically or mentally. Otherwise, Jesus would have known they were touching Him.

The disciples wanted to know why Jesus asked who had touched Him, since there were so many people crowded around Him. "And Jesus said, Somebody hath touched me: for I perceive that virtue is gone out of me" (Luke 8:46, KJV). "And he said unto her, Daughter, be of good comfort: thy faith hath made thee whole; go in peace" (Luke 8:48, KJV). The healing power of Jesus was overwhelmingly evident when faith was present.

PRAYER

Thank You, Jesus, for Your healing power and for Your love and kindness. Dear Heavenly Father, You know each one reading today's message. Should there be a need for healing, I pray You will speak the word and touch and heal every manner of sickness, both physical and mental. I also pray You will touch and heal every area of their lives. I pray for restored health, wholeness, and strong faith. I praise You, Jesus, and I lift You up. I ask for these blessings, in Your name. Amen.

Your Thoughts and Prayer Request

_____

_____

_____

_____

_____

_____

_____

_____

_____

_____

_____

_____

_____

_____

_____

_____

DAY 15

BREAKING CHAINS

*And when Herod would have brought him forth, the same
night Peter was sleeping between two soldiers, bound with two
chains: and the keepers before the door kept the prison. And,
behold, the angel of the Lord came upon him, and a light
shined in the prison: and he smote Peter on the side, and raised
him up, saying, Arise up quickly. And his chains fell off from
his hands. And the angel said unto him, Gird thyself, and
bind on thy sandals. And so he did. And he saith unto him,
Cast thy garment about thee, and follow me.*

—Acts 12:6–8 (KJV)

Don't allow chains to hold you down. I want today's message to inspire
each reader to break free from problems that have plagued families
for generations. By faith, believe God will set you free of those chains. There
was no mistake, but perfection, when the chains fell from Peter. Plus, God
sent an angel to instruct Peter and to escort him out of prison. "If the Son
therefore shall make you free, ye shall be free indeed" (John 8:36, KJV).

God breaks chains that are welded together by unforgiveness, hatred,
jealousy, negativity, and gossip. Today is the day to break free of those chains,
which starts with gaining knowledge about each one.

Forgiveness is letting go of anger and the thought of revenge. Unless a person seeks God's help, they will have no power to let go. The wrong that was done won't be forgotten, but because the person is letting go, the pain will be gone. The Mayo Clinic Staff said, "Forgiveness doesn't mean forgetting or excusing the harm done to you or making up with the person who caused the harm. Forgiveness brings a kind of peace that helps you go on with life"

The apostle Mark said, "And when you stand praying, if you hold anything against anyone, forgive them, so that your Father in heaven may forgive you your sins" (Mark 11:25, NIV). Forgiveness is a positive choice for physical well-being, mental well-being, and social well-being.

Wikipedia defines *hatred* as an "angry or resentful emotional response to certain people or ideas. Hatred is often associated with feelings of anger, disgust, and a disposition toward the source of hostility." According to A.J. Marsden, assistant professor of psychology and human services at Beacon College in Leesburg, Florida, "One reason we hate is because we fear things that are different from us."

I want to motivate each reader to love others, even when they exhibit poor behavior. You can love and pray for the person without loving the behavior. Ask the person if you may read them a Bible scripture, or simply recommend one. There's one I frequently recommend: "Whoever claims to love God yet hates a brother or sister is a liar. For whoever does not love their brother and sister, whom they have seen, cannot love God, whom they have not seen" (1 John 4:20, NIV). Hatred is the absence of love. A person can't love God and hate people.

Jealousy is being concerned with not having what someone else has. It's a feeling of insecurity. A jealous person has a low self-esteem, feels possessive of others, and thinks someone else looks better than they do. *Psychology Today* published an article that says, "There is no instant cure for jealousy.

But accepting that jealousy is normal, challenging negative thoughts, and practicing mindfulness may help reduce its pull."

It will be beneficial if each reader will compare themselves with what the Bible says about jealousy: "But if you have bitter envy and self-seeking in your hearts, do not boast and lie against the truth. This wisdom does not descend from above, but *is* earthly, sensual, demonic. For where envy and self-seeking *exist,* confusion and every evil thing *are* there" (James 3:14–16, NKJV).

Negativity encourages being disagreeable, expecting the worst, not verbalizing what is good, and saying things that may lower another person's self-esteem. If you've ever encountered a negative person, you might have wondered what's bothering them. Dr. Raj Raghunathan says, "It can be excruciatingly difficult to deal with negative people—people who bring your mood down with their pessimism, anxiety, and general sense of distrust. Constant exposure to such negativity can make deep inroads into your bank of positivity, leading you to either become negative—diffident, anxious, and distrustful—yourself, or to become indifferent, uncaring, or even mean toward the negative person."

If any of my readers recognize negativity operating in their lives, seek God's deliverance through prayer. If you know anyone who carries the trait of negativity, pray for that person. The apostle Paul said, " If we live in the Spirit, let us also walk in the Spirit" (Gal. 5:25, KJV). To live by the Spirit is to walk in faith and trust God and His Word in all areas of life. I thank God that I can choose what I say to and about others. God lets those who believe in Him to have the ability to choose to speak negative or positive things.

Chains will break when believers recognize what has been holding them captive. Speak to those chains by faith, and pray until they have fallen off your life. Praise God for deliverance, and get up. You are no longer bound.

PRAYER

Dear Heavenly Father, I pray for those who have been weighed down with the chains of unforgiveness, hatred, jealousy, and negativity. I pray You will remove these chains and set them free. Restore unto them the desire to walk with You, trust You, and believing in You. I pray You give them a mind to understand that reading the Bible is a light unto their feet and a brightened path to a victoriously blessed life. I ask for these blessings, in the name of Jesus. Amen.

Your Thoughts and Prayer Request

_____

_____

_____

_____

_____

_____

_____

_____

_____

_____

_____

_____

_____

_____

_____

_____

_____

_____

BEING FAITHFUL

God is faithful, by whom you were called into the fellowship of His Son, Jesus Christ our Lord.

—1 Corinthians 1:9 (NKJV)

I want those reading today's message to reflect on God's faithfulness, something I've thought about numerous times in my life. I grew up in a church environment that was rich in singing, testimonies, and praising the Lord. It was always a blessing to hear the prayers and listen to the members of the congregation testify about God's goodness and His faithfulness, something our church put a lot of emphasis on.

Jeremiah realized God's faithfulness after he had lamented over the Babylonians destroying his city. His lamenting expressed the pain and anguish he felt. He began feeling sorry for himself and for Jerusalem, the people he loved so much. After having this painful time to express his feelings, Jeremiah took a moment and composed his thoughts. In doing so, he remembered God's steadfast love. Jeremiah reminds himself that God has compassion, and he starts to find hope again. Thus, he writes, "*Through* the LORD's mercies we are not consumed, Because His compassions fail not. *They are* new every morning; Great *is* Your faithfulness" (Lam. 3:22–23, NKJV).

Daniel 6 reports that Daniel was faithful to God, and God was faithful to him. Notably, He gave Daniel favor in the sight of King Nebuchadnezzar. Daniel's wisdom, integrity, and faithfulness were recognized, meaning he could be trusted in a leadership position. Daniel's opponents became jealous and plotted against him, however, and they convinced King Nebuchadnezzar to sign a declaration stating that every citizen had to bow down and worship the golden image.

Daniel's opponents knew that Daniel would not follow this declaration, and they spied on him. In doing so, they witnessed Daniel kneeling and praying to God three times a day. King Nebuchadnezzar was told about Daniel's behavior, and reluctantly, the king ordered Daniel to be put into the lions' den.

During the night, the king could not sleep because he was worried about Daniel. In the morning he hurried to the lions' den, cried out, and asked Daniel if his God had delivered him. Daniel replied, "O king, live forever! My God sent His angel and shut the lions' mouths, so that they have not hurt me, because I was found innocent before Him; and also, O king, I have done no wrong before you" (Dan. 6:21–22 NKJV).

Daniel was a faithful assistant to King Nebuchadnezzar, but most important was his faithfulness to God. As a result of his faithfulness, God showed His powerful faithfulness to Daniel.

Being faithful is a commendable trait for all who follow Jesus and obey His Word.

PRAYER

I praise you, Jesus, for your faithfulness toward each reader. I praise You for everlasting life and for goodness, love, and kindness. I pray for today's message to be encouraging to all readers. I pray that each reader will evaluate their faithfulness and be willing to change in whichever area of their life they find deficient. I pray that friendships that are suffering from a lack of faithfulness to one another will be restored. I pray each reader's will to be faithful will be strengthened through reading Your Word, hearing Your Word, listening to songs about Your goodness, and hearing others talk of Your goodness. I ask for these blessings, in the name of Jesus. Amen.

Your Thoughts and Prayer Request

_____

_____

_____

_____

_____

_____

_____

_____

_____

_____

_____

_____

_____

_____

_____

_____

CHOICES

But the wisdom that is from above is first pure, then peaceable, gentle, willing to yield, full of mercy and good fruits, without partiality and without hypocrisy.

—James 3:17 (NKJV)

In Matthew 25:1–11, Jesus uses a parable to demonstrate wisdom and choices. In this parable, there were ten virgins. Five of them were wise and five were foolish. The five wise virgins made sure to keep their lamps filled with oil. Wisdom led them into staying ready. "And at midnight a cry was *heard:* 'Behold, the bridegroom is coming; go out to meet him!' Then all those virgins arose and trimmed their lamps. And the foolish said to the wise, 'Give us *some* of your oil, for our lamps are going out.' But the wise answered, saying, '*No,* lest there should not be enough for us and you; but go rather to those who sell, and buy for yourselves.' And while they went to buy, the bridegroom came, and those who were ready went in with him to the wedding; and the door was shut" (Matt. 25:6–10).

In this parable, readiness is identified. It's clear that God allows all who believe in Him to make the right choices and to act on those choices. Believers are also shown that the best choice is to give polite and honest replies with an explanation. Wisdom is important to the believer's life in verbal conversations and in decision making. In this parable, we witness the benefit of linking faith with patience, along with having trust, faith, and knowledge about the situation and having an ear to hear God's voice.

Zacchaeus was a rich tax collector whose purpose in life was to see Jesus. One day, he had this opportunity, but because he was of below-average height, he could not see over others. Quickly he made a choice. Zacchaeus ran ahead of the crowd and climbed up into a sycamore tree, knowing that Jesus would pass by.

When Jesus was near him, he looked up and told Zacchaeus to hurry down from the tree. This was an appointed day and time for Jesus to go and give salvation to Zacchaeus and his family. Zacchaeus told Jesus about his choice to give half of his possessions to the poor. He also made a choice to give back four times to anyone he had defrauded. Zacchaeus made a profitable choice; Jesus changed his life and saved his entire family. Zacchaeus received salvation because of the love of Jesus, not because he was a tax collector or because he climbed a tree.

Make the best choices in your life. Seek after Jesus as never before, through prayer and reading His Word, and make your choices based on what He says. This will be beneficial to you and your family. Should you reach a crossroads, listen for Jesus to give directions so that you make the right choices.

PRAYER

Thank you, Jesus, for today's message. I pray for increased spiritual wisdom for each reader to make the best choices in every area of their lives and in the lives of their loved ones. Good choices are an essential need as each reader walks by faith and not by sight. I ask for these blessings, in the mighty name of Jesus. Amen.

YOUR THOUGHTS AND PRAYER REQUEST

DAY 18

GOD MEETS NEEDS

> *Delight yourself also in the LORD, And He shall give you the desires of your heart. Commit your way to the LORD, Trust also in Him, And He shall bring it to pass.*
>
> —Psalm 37:4–5 (NKJV)

As a single mother raising two children, I would often pray and look for God's help, but with the natural eye. As time went by, the Holy Spirit helped me realize that God had been answering my prayers all along. Prayer and reading the Bible have helped me grow stronger in faith, in trusting God, and in knowing He has always heard my prayers. I know because every need for me and my children has been met.

In 1 Kings, God sent the prophet Elijah to Zarephath, so that God would meet the needs of a widow and her son. This woman had only a handful of flour and a little oil. Her plan was to prepare bread for her and her son and then die. Thankfully, due to divine intervention, this would not happen. God interrupted her plans so that her needs would be met.

Although the widow had no hope, she followed Elijah's instructions. His trust was steadfast in knowing that God meets needs. The Zarephath woman prepared a small cake for Elijah before preparing for her and her son. Due to her obedience, she and her son had plenty to eat for a long time. "The bin of flour was not used up, nor did the jar of oil run dry, according to the word of the LORD which He spoke by Elijah" (1 Kings 17:16, NKJV). She became a believer of and witness to the fact that God meets needs.

With continued faith and trust in God, Elijah listened to the needs of a poor woman. She explained to him that her husband, who had been one of God's servants, had died. She told Elijah that the creditor was going to take her two sons from her to be slaves. Elijah asked, "Tell me, what do you have in the house?" (2 Kings 4:2, NKJV). She only had a jar of oil. Elijah instructed her to borrow empty vessels from anyone she could find. After she did so, Elijah told her to go into her house and shut the door. His final instruction was for her to pour the oil into all the vessels and to put the full ones to the side. The oil never ran out until there were no more vessels to pour it into. Then Elijah said to her "Go, sell the oil and pay your debt; and you *and* your sons live on the rest" (2 Kings 4:7, NKJV).

Trust God to meet all of your needs, no matter what your natural eyes are telling you or what you think might be difficult. Have faith and believe that God will do what seems impossible from our point of view; anything is possible with God.

PRAYER

Dear Heavenly Father, I humbly come before You with praise and thanksgiving. Thank You for meeting the needs of each one who is reading today's message. I pray for blessings in their life. I pray for increased faith and that You will meet all of their needs. You see and know the heart's desire of each one reading today's message. I pray for their strength and trust in You in all areas of life. I ask for these blessings, in the name of Jesus. Amen.

YOUR THOUGHTS AND PRAYER REQUEST

The Secret Place

He who dwells in the secret place of the Most High Shall abide under the shadow of the Almighty.

—Psalm 91:1 (NKJV)

T oday's message is to enlighten all readers about emotional and psychological abuse. When someone mentions abuse, most of the time physical abuse leaps to mind. Physical abuse leaves outward marks such as bald spots, darkness around the eyes, or bruising of the skin. These can be treated with a bandage, an ice pack, or medication. Most of the time, however, emotional and psychological abuse leave no outward marks.

Pictures can be taken of physical abuse for visual proof. Also, your family, coworkers, and friends might notice the marks. Even a mirror will tell the truth. Not so with emotional and psychological abuse, the results of which include anxiety, feelings of belittlement, confusion, depression, doubt, loneliness, or loss of a loved one. Unless the one who is suffering verbalizes these emotions, most of the time the only ones who will know are the victim and God. "Behold, the LORD's hand is not shortened, that it cannot save; neither his ear heavy, that it cannot hear" (Isa. 59:1, KJV).

Those believing and trusting in the Lord are encouraged to go to their secret place and talk to Jesus. Your secret place is a place where you feel free to tell all, a place where only God can hear your worries, your fears, and your despair. He will be listening with love and compassion; He is your hope for a better future.

On October 4, 2016, Pastor Joseph Prince's message was titled "What is the Secret Place Mentioned in Psalm 91?" He said, "God is aware and it is ok to cry. Only He has the answer. Only in Him we can find protection. Shadow is protection, in Hebrew."

David said, "He who dwells in the secret place of the Most High Shall abide under the shadow of the Almighty. I will say of the LORD, '*He is* my refuge and my fortress; My God, in Him I will trust" (Ps. 91:1–2, NKJV).

I want to give hope, strengthen, and encouragement to those reading this message so that they'll go to God in prayer; go to your quiet area, your quiet place. Tell Him all about the emotional, verbal, or physical abuse you're going through. Talk about it with Jesus. If it's depression, tell Him. If you're dealing with anger, talk to God about it. If fear is consuming your life, tell Him all about it. If your conversation with God becomes overwhelming and you start to cry, it's all right. God hears your cry.

David tells believers that oppression will stop: "LORD, You have heard the desire of the humble; You will prepare their heart; You will cause Your ear to hear, To do justice to the fatherless and the oppressed, That the man of the earth may oppress no more" (Ps. 10:16–18, NKJV).

According to *Merriam Webster's Dictionary*, *oppression* means "unjust or cruel exercise of authority or power." This is not needed. It's unfair, abusive, and cruel to the person experiencing it.

I'm reminded of Hagar. She was a servant to Sarah, Abraham's wife, and oppressed by both her and Abraham. Because Sarah was childless, she instructed Hagar to sleep with her eighty-five-year-old husband, Abraham, so that he and Sarah could have a child.

Hagar gave birth to a son and named him Ishmael. Fourteen years after the birth of Ishmael, Sarah gave birth to Isaac. At this time, Abraham was one hundred years of age. One day Sarah witnessed Ishmael making fun of Isaac. So, she told Abraham to send Hagar and Ishmael away from their home. After Abraham gave Hagar some bread and water, he sent her and Ishmael away.

Hagar and Ishmael wandered in the wilderness. It was an untamed and uncultivated land; there were no others around. This became Hagar's secret place. She and her son had no more water to drink. So, Hagar put Ishmael under a shrub and moved away from him. Next, she started to cry and tell God about her disappointments in life. I believe she may have told God about how Sarah and Abraham had oppressed her, how they had control over her life. Hagar believed no one would hear her cries. But she and her son were not alone; God saw them and heard Hagar. He sent an angel to tell her not to fear. The angel told her that Ishmael would grow up to be the ancestor of great nations.

Miracles are manifested in the secret place of a person's life. God worked a miracle for Hagar. He opened her eyes to see the well of water God created for her and her son. God made the wilderness a livable environment for Ishmael to grow up in. He became a skilled archer and married an Egyptian woman chosen by his mother, Hagar.

Let your secret place be where you have a relationship with God, through prayer, through praise, and through the reading of His Word.

PRAYER

Dear Father, I pray You will meet the physical and spiritual needs of each one reading this message. I pray You will give them wisdom and knowledge about how they can go into their secret place. I pray You will heal those who have been mistreated, who are depressed, who have been emotionally abused, who harbor the pain and memories of physical abuse, and who are angry. I ask You to tear down those walls of loneliness, pull up doubt from the root, deliver them from oppression, and heal all their physical ailments. I pray for restoration in all areas of their life. I ask for these blessings, in the name of Jesus. Amen.

YOUR THOUGHTS AND PRAYER REQUEST

_____

_____

_____

_____

_____

_____

_____

_____

_____

_____

_____

_____

_____

_____

_____

_____

_____

HAVE PATIENCE

*And let us not grow weary while doing good, for in due season
we shall reap if we do not lose heart.*

—Galatians 6:9 (NKJV)

There is a definite distinction between being weary and being tired. Being tired means needing to rest or sleep. Weariness means that one's strength has been exhausted. It's meaningless, excessive, rooted in unbelief and toil.

God does not want those who believe in Him to toil. He said to, "Consider the lilies, how they grow: they neither toil nor spin; and yet I say to you, even Solomon in all his glory was not arrayed like one of these" (Luke 12:27, NKJV). Praying to our Heavenly Father does not produce weariness. Having patience with faith during prayer produces results for those needing a breakthrough in their spiritual life. "Now faith is the substance of things hoped for, the evidence of things not seen" (Heb. 11:1, KJV).

It is better to sow good; do good to all with sincere and honest thoughts. God knows the heart; He knows every intention, whether good or bad. Therefore, sowing good will be beneficial for your reaping season. A person will reap what they have sown. Have patience when sowing to be certain of a righteous heart. Don't do something for another in a hurry or just to be recognized. Sow from your heart, patiently.

God instructed Isaiah to write about having patience, to endure like the eagle. Isaiah wrote, "But those who wait on the LORD Shall renew *their* strength; They shall mount up with wings like eagles, They shall run and not be weary, They shall walk and not faint" (Isa. 40:31, NKJV). Patiently waiting on God is essential for all who live a righteous life. "Therefore we also, since we are surrounded by so great a cloud of witnesses, let us lay aside every weight, and the sin which so easily ensnares *us,* and let us run with endurance the race that is set before us, looking unto Jesus, the author and finisher of *our* faith, who for the joy that was set before Him endured the cross, despising the shame, and has sat down at the right hand of the throne of God" (Heb. 12:1–2, NKJV).

Paul gives guidance on having patience when preparing for and running this spiritual race. To start, believers are to let go of all that is weighing them down. In the natural race, runners do not carry weights. Their running garments consist of a light sleeveless shirt and light comfortable shorts or pants. Let go of worry, disappointment, anxiety, depression, bitterness, hatred, jealousy, covetousness, anger, and thoughts of failure. Let go of grudges and forgive those who have misused you. Let go of all that is weighing you down, and wait for God to direct you. "Trust in the LORD with all your heart, And lean not on your own understanding; In all your ways acknowledge Him, And He shall direct your paths" (Prov. 3:5–6, NKJV).

One of the defining characteristics of an eagle is strength. God wants us to be strong in our belief, in our faith, and in our endurance through the difficult times. The eagle has patience to wait for its strength to be restored, and it has exceptionally strong vision. God wants believers to have strong spiritual vision to focus on what He will do to renew our strength, not on what we can't do.

The eagle will use the wind of a storm to get to safety as it patiently soars through the sky. When the storms of life are raging, Jesus is your hope. He is the wind that lifts you during the difficult times. He is able to keep you steadfast and unmovable in spite of the bad choices you may have made. Move away from those choices, that storm, and have patience as you pursue the right choices that will result in success, not failure.

Prayer

Dear Heavenly Father, I pray that today's message will encourage and teach readers about having patience. I pray they have patience to wait on You. I pray You will give patience when sincere seeds have been planted. I pray for an understanding about reaping good when good has been sown. I pray for each reader to develop patience as their strength is being renewed. I pray for strong spiritual vision to see, by faith, to run and not grow weary. I ask these blessings, in the mighty name of Jesus. Amen.

Your Thoughts and Prayer Request

_____

_____

_____

_____

_____

_____

_____

_____

_____

_____

_____

_____

_____

_____

_____

_____

_____

_____

SPIRITUAL NOURISHMENT

But blessed is the one who trusts in the LORD, whose confidence
is in him. They will be like a tree planted by the water that
sends out its roots by the stream. It does not fear when heat
comes; its leaves are always green. It has no worries in a year
of drought and never fails to bear fruit.

—Jeremiah 17:7–8 (NIV)

Trees that are nourished by ample water and sun will grow healthier than trees that are not. When they grow next to water, there will be no concern about a water shortage. Jeremiah provides this metaphor to explain the benefits of growing near the water of everlasting life, where the Son of God shines upon those who believe and trust in Him. Jesus supplies spiritual nourishment to believers. Therefore, the behavior of those who follow Jesus should exhibit love as well as care for others, with a spiritual life that encompasses prayer. Spiritual nourishment will include hearing God's Word being preached and taught. Coupled with studying the Bible, and applying it to life.

In Acts 8:26–35, Philip imparts spiritual nourishment to an Ethiopian man. An angel told Philip to go to the desert. When Philip arrived at his destination, he saw the Ethiopian man, a eunuch with considerable authority under Candace, queen of the Ethiopians. He was in Jerusalem to worship. Philip observed the eunuch sitting in his chariot and reading the teachings of Isaiah, so he asked the eunuch whether he understood the teaching. He answered, "How can I, unless someone guides me?" (Acts 8:31, NKJV). This question gave permission for Philip to impart spiritual nourishment to the eunuch, after which he accepted God's Word because Philip had made it clear to him.

The fruits believers produce are not of their own doing. They are the result of being filled with the Holy Spirit, who encourages prayer with faith. I want to inspire believers to stay planted by the river of living water for continual spiritual nourishment. By doing this, your roots will go deep and have an anchored connection with Jesus, who is the living water needed for spiritual nourishment.

Reaching out to Jesus is similar to the way the roots of a tree grow when planted near water. Believers are to be connected to Jesus, the way branches are connected to a tree trunk. Your leaves will be green and your fruits of the Spirit will be healthy. Jesus said, "If you abide in Me, and My words abide in you, you will ask what you desire, and it shall be done for you" (John 15:7, NKJV).

Prayer

Dear Heavenly Father, I pray You will give encouragement to those who are reading *Calming Streams.* I pray today's message will overflow with spiritual encouragement. I pray for each reader to learn how to stay planted near the water of life. I praise You, Jesus, for being the spiritual water of life for all who believe. I praise You for being the water by which every branch of their lives is nourished. I pray You will nourish each with Your Word. I pray for the character of each believer to emulate Your character. I ask for these blessings, in the mighty name of Jesus. Amen.

YOUR THOUGHTS AND PRAYER REQUEST

_____

_____

_____

_____

_____

_____

_____

_____

_____

_____

_____

_____

_____

_____

_____

_____

THE HOLY SPIRIT

*But the Helper, the Holy Spirit, whom the Father will send
in My name, He will teach you all things, and bring to your
remembrance all things that I said to you.*

—John 14:26 (NKJV)

The Holy Spirit is a gift given to those who believe that Jesus died on the cross and, three days later, got up from the grave. The only individual requirement for receiving this gift is believing that Jesus is who He says He is. Born-again believers are to listen to the guidance of the Holy Spirit, according to the fruits of the Spirit. He fills those who choose to believe in Jesus, the Son of God, with His love. "For God so loved the world that He gave His only begotten Son, that whoever believes in Him should not perish but have everlasting life" (John 3:16, NKJV).

Jesus gave instructions, which included the Holy Spirit: "Go therefore and make disciples of all the nations, baptizing them in the name of the Father and of the Son and of the Holy Spirit" (Matt. 28:19, NKJV),

In 2 Corinthians, Jesus teaches Paul about the fellowship of the Holy Spirit: "The grace of the Lord Jesus Christ, and the love of God, and the communion of the Holy Spirit *be* with you all. Amen" (2 Cor. 13:14, NKJV). These words are a stamp of approval for all believers to acknowledge three different persons: God the Father, Jesus the Son, and the Holy Spirit. The Holy Spirit helps and comforts those who believe in Jesus.

Being born again, filled with the Holy Spirit, is accomplished by faith. The Holy Spirit is given to empower those who believe. It assists with living a holy life and being a fruitful witness. "The fruit of the Spirit is love, joy, peace, longsuffering, kindness, goodness, faithfulness, gentleness, self-control" (Gal. 5:22–23, NKJV).

Love: The Bible says to love the Lord your God with all your heart. The heart encompasses the emotions, the mind, the will, and the conscience. When we have done something wrong, this fruit lets us know. If we have wronged another believer, we need to ask them for forgiveness. Remember to pray and ask God to forgive you, and read scriptures pertaining to forgiving. "Love is patient, love is kind. It does not envy, it does not boast, it is not proud. It does not dishonor others, it is not self-seeking, it is not easily angered, it keeps no record of wrongs" (1 Cor. 13:4–5, NKJV).

Joy: When God restores the areas of your life that you gave up on, you will experience joy. Joy is the manifestation of God restoring areas of a broken life and giving you the spiritual strength to move forward. "Until now you have asked nothing in My name. Ask, and you will receive, that your joy may be full" (John 16:24, NKJV). "The joy of the LORD is your strength" (Neh. 8:10, NKJV).

Peace: Without Jesus, peace is often thought of as a quiet or calm life. But with Jesus, peace transcends into the spiritual realm. This fruit of the Holy Spirit will keep you in perfect peace when you believe and trust God. There may be confusion, strife, and trouble all around you, but trust the peace that God gives. "Peace I leave with you; my peace I give you. I do not give to you as the world gives. Do not let your hearts be troubled and do not be afraid" (John 14:23, NIV). Never doubt that God will keep you in perfect peace when your mind is stayed on Him.

Longsuffering: This is one of the positive traits Paul lists for believers to prayerfully achieve: "Therefore, as *the* elect of God, holy and beloved, put on tender mercies, kindness, humility, meekness, longsuffering" (Col. 3:12, NKJV). In life, believers will suffer from being mistreated, sometimes for long periods (or what seem like long periods). Nevertheless, those who believe in Jesus have hope because they know and trust God. With this fruit, the Holy Spirit will lead and guide us through longsuffering. After you have experienced suffering, you can encourage others with your testimony.

Kindness: When Jesus walked this earth, He set an example of kindness, no matter the color of one's skin, their physical appearance, whether they were wealthy or poor, or where they lived. Jesus showed love and kindness to the leper, to the lame, to the blind, to the possessed, and to the hungry, and He gave hearing to the deaf. All were treated the same way. "Be kind and compassionate to one another, forgiving each other, just as in Christ God forgave you" (Eph. 4:32, NIV).

Goodness: The fruit of goodness should not be equated with getting recognition. The Holy Spirit leads the believer to do good without being recognized because we are to be like Jesus, and He is good. He is our refuge and our strength; He will never change. We are to pray for the sick, feed the hungry, give to the poor, teach God's Word, and be a light that sits upon a hill. Paul said, "Therefore, as we have opportunity, let us do good to all people, especially to those who belong to the family of believers" (Gal. 6:10, NIV).

Faithfulness: God has been and wants to continue to be the reliable source of loyalty and faithfulness in a believer's life. In other words, you can depend on Him, and the Holy Spirit helps believers recognize that. As you continue to be a faithful believer in God and to follow His Word, the Holy Spirit will remind you to be faithful to others. "For the LORD is good and his love endures forever; his faithfulness continues through all generations" (Ps. 100:5, NIV).

Gentleness: This fruit presents a kind and caring spirit toward others. One day, during Jesus' ministry, a man covered with leprosy approached Jesus and asked if He would heal him. He had faith that Jesus was a healer, but still wondered whether He was willing to heal him because of his condition. "Then Jesus, moved with compassion, stretched out *His* hand and touched him, and said to him, 'I am willing; be cleansed'" (Mark 1:41, NKJV). Jesus showed the importance of being gentle with His touch and through His spoken words. "With all lowliness and gentleness, with long-suffering, bearing with one another in love" (Eph. 4:2, NKJV).

Self-Control: This fruit helps believers become aware of their words and actions. Believers are to build up, not tear down, another person. We are to listen to the needs of others and give support. "Finally, brethren, whatever things are true, whatever things *are* noble, whatever things *are* just, whatever things *are* pure, whatever things *are* lovely, whatever things *are* of good report, if *there is* any virtue and if *there is* anything praiseworthy—meditate on these things" (Phil. 4:8, NKJV).

PRAYER

Dear Heavenly Father, I come humbly before You. I praise You for Your Son and for the Holy Spirit. I pray that everyone reading today's message will experience greater love, joy, peace, longsuffering, kindness, goodness, faithfulness, gentleness, and self-control. I ask that You will teach each one reading today's message about the Holy Spirit's ability to move them forward into a more filling and prosperous life. I ask for these blessings, in the mighty name of Jesus. Amen.

YOUR THOUGHTS AND PRAYER REQUEST

_____

_____

_____

_____

_____

_____

_____

_____

_____

_____

_____

_____

_____

_____

_____

_____

GOD KNOWS YOUR HEART

But the LORD said to Samuel, "Do not look at his appearance or at his physical stature, because I have refused him. For the LORD does not see as man sees; for man looks at the outward appearance, but the LORD looks at the heart.

—1 Samuel 16:7 (NKJV)

God knows your heart, every tear that falls from your eyes, and every second you've spent praying for a loved one to make the right choices. When you pray, don't worry about how you look or whether you pronounce every word correctly. Just say what's on your heart. If your heart has been broken, God knows. Just talk to Him; tell Jesus all about it.

Your spiritual heart is the arena of thoughts, emotions, and desires; it's the soul. A heart can be totally shattered when hope for a better life starts to dissipate. When this happens, God knows. Trust Him and have faith that He will restore to you what the devil has stolen.

If a precious glass vase is shattered, pieces of glass will scatter everywhere. You may try to piece the vase back together, but all the imperfections will show, and there may still be missing pieces. God takes time to heal and restore the pieces of a broken heart. He takes away despair and replaces it with hope. God heals areas of emotional pain that doctors cannot diagnose.

When will you know you've been healed? When will you know you've been restored? You will know, because when you think about those areas that were shattered and pieces that were missing, you won't feel the sting. The pain is gone. Jesus "heals the brokenhearted And binds up their wounds" (Ps. 147:3, NKJV).

Job 1:13–22 tells the unfortunate account of a man whose heart was broken. Job lost all his sons and daughters, his servants, as well as his sheep and camels. But Job received no support or encouraging words. His wife told him to curse God and die. His three friends told him he did something wrong.

But even though Job's heart was broken, he prayed and kept his faith in God. As a result, God healed and restored Job's broken heart flawlessly. God also restored his fortune more than Job could have ever thought or imagined. "Now the LORD blessed the latter *days* of Job more than his beginning; for he had fourteen thousand sheep, six thousand camels, one thousand yoke of oxen, and one thousand female donkeys. He also had seven sons and three daughters" (Job 42:12).

PRAYER

Thank you, Jesus, for today's message. I give You praise for who You are. I praise You for knowing the heart of everyone reading today's message. Should there be a reader who has a broken heart, I pray You will restore, bind up, and heal in the mighty name of Jesus. I pray You will rebuke fear, cast out doubt, and inspire hope and strong faith to be present in this believer's life. I thank You, Jesus, and I believe it is being done. In the mighty name of Jesus. Amen.

YOUR THOUGHTS AND PRAYER REQUEST

Letting Go
of the Past

*Brethren, I do not count myself to have apprehended; but
one thing I do, forgetting those things which are behind and
reaching forward to those things which are ahead, I press
toward the goal for the prize of the upward call of God in
Christ Jesus.*

—Philippians 3:23 (NKJV)

While in prison, the apostle Paul wrote to the congregation of Philippi to encourage them to leave the past behind and look to their future. Today's message is to encourage all readers to stop thinking about their past regrets, about what could have been, and about what might have happened "if only." Let go of the thoughts of when you were mistreated and forgive those who have hurt you.

Praise God for today. Praise Him for bringing you out of the difficult situations the devil was using to drain your strength and cause you to walk in a cycle of sadness. Praise God for what He has done and for what He is going to do. In Psalms, David used faith to persevere during trying times. He said, "I waited patiently for the LORD; And He inclined to me, And heard my cry. He also brought me up out of a horrible pit, Out of the miry clay, And set my feet upon a rock, *And* established my steps" (Ps. 40:1–2, NKJV). David let go of the past and fixed his mind on God, knowing He would deliver him.

In the Old Testament, God tells us about a woman who could not let go of the past. We don't know her name, but Jesus refers to her as Lot's wife. God told Lot He was going to destroy the city they were living in and instructed him to take his wife, his children, and not to look back. Lot followed God's instructions. Unfortunately, his wife could not let go of the past and looked back, thinking about what was left behind. When she looked back, "she became a pillar of salt" (Gen. 19:26, NKJV). God wants every believer to know He wants to bless you and your future. The past is behind you. With faith, prayer, and reading God's Word, look to your future.

PRAYER

Dear Heavenly Father, I pray You will bless the future of all who are reading today's message. I pray each reader will let go of thinking about their past misfortunes and think about their future. I pray for a renewed mind for all those who have been regretting their past. I pray for believers who have been stuck due to hurt, pain, mistreatment, and disappointment. I pray for each believer to pick up one foot at a time and step into the blessings You have for their lives. I pray each believer will grab hold of newness. I pray for physical strength; mental strength; faith in You, Lord; and focus on what will be done in their lives. I ask for these blessings in the mighty name of Jesus. Amen.

Your Thoughts and Prayer Request

Be Steadfast

My brethren, count it all joy when you fall into various trials, knowing that the testing of your faith produces patience. But let patience have its perfect work, that you may be perfect and complete, lacking nothing.

—James 1:2–4 (NKJV)

Webster's Dictionary defines being steadfast as being "firmly fixed in place" or "firm in belief, determination." The Lord did not say that believing and trusting in Him would mean a life of prosperity and no hardships or struggles.

The prophet Jeremiah witnessed God destroying the city of Jerusalem, because the Jews rejected Jesus. Jeremiah wrote the book of Lamentations as a lament for what occurred. Lament is what Jeremiah felt, sorrow and loss for his people. Nevertheless, Jeremiah stood steadfast and believed in Jesus as the author and finisher of his faith. He knew God's steadfast love would never stop and His mercies would never end. Rather, they would be new every morning. Jeremiah knew God's faithfulness would always be great. "*Through* the LORD's mercies we are not consumed, Because His compassions fail not. *They are* new every morning; Great *is* Your faithfulness" (Lam. 3:22–23, NKJV).

As a high school student, I did research on the palm tree. I lived in a city where, at times, the wind would swoop down from the mountains. It was not a breeze; it was steadily strong. It would push against anyone in its path, and it was powerful enough to rearrange landscaping. If I were waiting for the school bus on a windy morning, I would find myself jumping around, trying to avoid the tumbleweeds. All who waited for the school bus were attacked by many tumbleweeds, small, medium, and large.

One day, my focus turned to the palm trees. I saw tall, graceful trees swaying in the wind. I thought they were going to break, but they never did. My curiosity led me to write a book report about palm trees, and I discovered they were strong and steadfast in nature. They could also bend up to forty or more degrees without snapping. To this day, I continue to look at palm trees and appreciate their strong and graceful stance.

When I was fourteen, I accepted Jesus into my life and was filled with the Holy Spirit. I imagined an almost perfect life. I didn't know at the time that I would encounter numerous trials, disappointments, and grief, but God has always given me strength. Through reading and hearing His Word, my faith in Him has helped me to be steadfast. Like the palm tree, there were times I've had to bend, but because of my faith and trust in God, I was able to stand up straight again. Now, I can relate to David when he said, "I will lift up my eyes to the hills—From whence comes my help? My help *comes* from the LORD, Who made heaven and earth" (Ps. 121:1–2, NKJV).

PRAYER

Dear Jesus, I pray You will bless each one reading today's message. I pray each one will be steadfast and have peace in every trial and tribulation. I pray for encouragement and strength. I pray You will strengthen their memory of Your Word and memories of Your goodness. Bless each one to seek after steadiness with strong faith. I praise You for Your steadfast love and care. I pray for each reader to give You praise each day in every situation. I ask for these blessings, in the mighty name of Jesus. Amen.

YOUR THOUGHTS AND PRAYER REQUEST

_____

_____

_____

_____

_____

_____

_____

_____

_____

_____

_____

_____

_____

_____

_____

_____

DAY 26

RESTORATION

But those who wait on the LORD Shall renew their strength;
They shall mount up with wings like eagles, They shall run and
not be weary, They shall walk and not faint.

—Isaiah 40:31 (NKJV)

God wants believers to know He is a restorer of their loss. When God restores, He will make life better than it was before. In Jeremiah 30, God lets Israel know He is going to bless their future, both physically and spiritually.

Today's message is to remind all who believe and trust God that He will heal the wounds and scars of life we sustain when going through trials and tribulations. God will restore more than you lost. The improvement of your life will exceed what you can ever think or imagine. Hold on to your strong prayer life. Read the Bible with an understanding, and most significantly, your faith. David said, "He restores my soul; He leads me in the paths of righteousness For His name's sake" (Ps. 23:3, KJV).

Remember the Samaritan woman who went to draw water from Jacob's well. She was not thinking about her character being restored when she went to the community well. She chose to go to the well around noon, which was a hot time of the day, to avoid being around the other women, knowing they went in the early morning and evening when it was cool. The Samaritan woman had no idea Jesus would be waiting at the well for her and that respect would be restored to her. Jesus knew all about her lack, her hurt, how she lived, and who she was living with.

When the Samaritan woman arrived at the well, Jesus requested a drink of water. She told Jesus that Samaritan women don't associate with Jews. But this fact did not matter to Jesus, and He let her know that He was the living water, even though He did not have a vessel with Him. However, the Samaritan woman continued her conversation with Jesus by asking how she could get this living water. Jesus answered, "Whoever drinks of this water will thirst again, but whoever drinks of the water that I shall give him will never thirst. But the water that I shall give him will become in him a fountain of water springing up into everlasting life" (John 4:13–14, NKJV).

The Samaritan woman's life would never be the same. Believing brought restoration to her life. Her encounter at the well changed her thinking from hopelessness to hope. She'd been fundamentally untrusting, but she was transformed into a person who trusted. When the entire city recognized the change in her character, they were excited to meet Jesus.

Before meeting Jesus, the Samaritan woman did not have a testimony. After hearing and believing Jesus, she had a testimony, and her character was a witness. Jesus is waiting for you. Be who you are and meet with Him through your prayers.

PRAYER

I praise You, Jesus, for Your love and kindness. I praise You for those reading today's message, and I pray for healing in every area of their lives. I pray You will bind negative thinking and release positive thoughts. I pray for restoration and increase to begin in the life of each reader today. I pray for every need to be met. I pray for faith and hope to be restored. I pray for restored spiritual vision, restored possibilities, restored love for family, and a restored desire to read Your Word and attend church. I pray for restored dreams, restored honor, restored positive thinking, and restored hope. I ask for these blessings, in the name of Jesus. Amen.

YOUR THOUGHTS AND PRAYER REQUEST

TRUE FOUNDATION

But he who heard and did nothing is like a man who built a house on the earth without a foundation, against which the stream beat vehemently; and immediately it fell. And the ruin of that house was great.

—Luke 6:49 (NKJV)

When building a house, it is wise to start with a solid foundation, which should hold steady during times of wind, rain, storms, hurricanes, and tornadoes. Even if the framework becomes weakened or damaged, the foundation should remain strong. Building a spiritual life should start with a foundation that will hold during life's trials, tribulations, and times of enormous trouble and suffering.

Matthew 7:24–27 provides reasons why believers should build on a solid foundation. In this chapter, Jesus was on a mountain, teaching numerous followers. Before He finished, He told a parable about a wise man and a foolish man. The wise man built his house on rock, and the foolish man built his house on sand.

When the building was completed, there came a time of rain, floods, and wind. Because the foolish man chose to build on sand, his house fell because the rain and the floods moved the sand and the foundation along with it. Plus, the wind beat against the structure, causing it to tear away with the foundation and crumble.

But the wise man, who chose to build his house on the rock, had no need to worry because he had built his house on a solid foundation. So, he had rest and peace all the while his house was standing strong against the winds, the rain, and the floods.

Jesus was telling the crowd to make wise choices about who they will put their trust in. He was telling them He is that solid foundation to help and keep those who believe in Him through sickness, worry, grief, pain, and disappointments. Jesus will strengthen you and He will never leave you. "Therefore everyone who hears these words of mine and puts them into practice is like a wise man who built his house on the rock" (Matt. 17:24, NIV).

My hope is that today's message will encourage and inspire all to build their lives on God's Word, with faith. Choose to be wise; trust and do what God says.

PRAYER

Dear Heavenly Father, as I stand on a solid foundation, I know that all other ground is sinking sand. You are the rock that each and every person reading today's message is to stand on. Up on this rock I praise You, Lord. I lift up Your will to be done in the life of each reader. I praise You for Your loving-kindness. I praise You for unmerited favor. I thank You for being a friend. I thank You for Your Son and for the Holy Spirit. I pray for calmness in every storm of life. I pray for each one reading today's message to hear Your Word, to read Your Word, and to live by Your Word. I pray You give them strength and endurance during the trials and tribulations of their lives. I pray You give them spiritual eyesight to discern Your will. I pray You will give them excellent physical health. These blessings I ask for, in the mighty name of Jesus. Amen.

YOUR THOUGHTS AND PRAYER REQUEST

_____

_____

_____

_____

_____

_____

_____

_____

_____

_____

_____

_____

_____

_____

_____

DAY 28

ANXIETY INTERRUPTS PEACE

> *Be anxious for nothing, but in everything by prayer and supplication, with thanksgiving, let your requests be made known to God; and the peace of God, which surpasses all understanding, will guard your hearts and minds through Christ Jesus.*
>
> —Philippians 4:6–7 (NKJV)

Today I'm sharing a message I hope will resonate with those whose peace is being interrupted by anxiety. While this may be an uncommon topic, those reading today's message will acquire more knowledge about it, which will benefit their physical health as well as their spiritual growth.

Micah Abraham said, "The ability to cope with life stress is a skill. It's something that can be lost. The bible teaches the idea that, while there are many ways to learn to cope with stress, the most powerful is simply believing in God. Belief and faith in the Lord are the only place one needs to turn to learn how to cope with stress, because God delivers that help each and every day."

The July 2020 issue of *Psychology Today,* featured an article entitled "Why We Feel Anxiety", by Noam Shpancer. He reported that Anxiety is a persistent apprehension regarding potential future threats. Whereas fear is associated with an immediate "fight or flight" response that produces terror, anxiety provokes a "stop, look and listen" response and produces anticipatory worry. In other words, anxiety is what one feels on the night before the big battle. Fear is what is felt during the battle.

The American Psychological Association published an article titled "Anxiety". In this article it was argued that Anxiety is an emotion characterized by feelings of tension, worried thoughts and physical changes, like increased blood pressure. People with anxiety disorders usually have recurring intrusive thoughts or concerns. They may avoid certain situations, due to worry. Also, they may have physical symptoms such as sweating, trembling, dizziness, or a rapid heartbeat.

The Bible says anxiety is the result of uncertainty and causes the believer to experience fears and worries. The remedy for those who believe and trust in God, which consists of having a consistent prayer life, reading the Bible, and listening to the preached and taught Word of God, can interrupt these feelings.

Paul wrote to the church in Philippi and told them that as soon as anxiety is recognized, believers are to pray and speak to the situation. You can change the situation by speaking words of faith, for example, "I trust in the Lord with all my heart, and I will not lean on my understanding. God is my hope and my salvation in whom I trust. I will always know that God sees me and knows all about what I am going through. God is doing what He knows is best for me. I can do all things through God who gives me strength. God increases my strength and encourages me to do right."

When you declare these blessings loudly, peace will replace anxiety because the devil will have to stop feeding negative thoughts to your mind. David said, "Let the words of my mouth and the meditation of my heart Be acceptable in Your sight, O LORD, my strength and my Redeemer" (Ps. 19:14, NKJV).

Reading God's Word has a powerful effect on the lives of believers. "For God has not given us a spirit of fear, but of power and of love and of a sound mind" (2 Tim. 1:7, NKJV). God doesn't want those who believe in Him to have anxiety but to have peace. He lets all know this in John. "Peace I leave with you, My peace I give to you; not as the world gives do I give to you. Let not your heart be troubled, neither let it be afraid" (John 14:27, NKJV).

David said, "Yea, though I walk through the valley of the shadow of death, I will fear no evil; For You are with me; Your rod and Your staff, they comfort me" (Ps. 23:4, NKJV).

Matthew said, "Therefore do not worry about tomorrow, for tomorrow will worry about its own things. Sufficient for the day *is* its own trouble" (Matt. 6:34, NKJV).

Luke gives these instructions: "Therefore I say to you, do not worry about your life, what you will eat; nor about the body, what you will put on. Life is more than food, and the body *is more* than clothing. Consider the ravens, for they neither sow nor reap, which have neither storehouse nor barn; and God feeds them. Of how much more value are you than the birds? And which of you by worrying can add one cubit to his stature? If you then are not able to do *the* least, why are you anxious for the rest?" (Luke 12:22–26, NKJV).

If you don't know the words to say when praying to be delivered from anxiety, let the Holy Spirit plead your case to God: "Likewise the Spirit also helps in our weaknesses. For we do not know what we should pray for as we ought, but the Spirit Himself makes intercession for us with groanings which cannot be uttered. Now He who searches the hearts knows what the mind of the Spirit *is,* because He makes intercession for the saints according to *the will of* God" (Rom. 8:26–27, NKJV).

The apostle Paul encourages believers through his testimony. He was a witness to having peace in the midst of trials and tribulations, as anxiety attempted to interrupt his peace. Paul wrote about being in jail, without food for many days, beaten, stoned, and facing danger at sea. Instead of yielding to anxiety, Paul remained focused on God's promises.

PRAYER

Dear Heavenly Father, today, I am praying for those who are trapped in the web of fear and of feeling alone, as their minds race with the uncertainties of life. I am praying for those who have accepted You as their Lord and Savior but are not able to rest. I pray You will release their minds from anxiety. I pray You will replace fear with calmness and anxiety with peace and bring comfort and healing to their bodies. I pray You will give them confidence and strength with strong faith. I ask for these blessings, in the mighty name of Jesus. Amen.

YOUR THOUGHTS AND PRAYER REQUEST

_____

_____

_____

_____

_____

_____

_____

_____

_____

_____

_____

_____

_____

_____

_____

_____

_____

DAY 29

REMEMBER GOD'S BLESSINGS

I will meditate on the glorious splendor of Your majesty, And on Your wondrous works. Men shall speak of the might of Your awesome acts, And I will declare Your greatness. They shall utter the memory of Your great goodness, And shall sing of Your righteousness.

—Psalm 145:5–7 (NKJV)

Today's message will encourage all who are reading to remember God's blessings. I hope you will take some time each day to relax, close your eyes, and meditate about how good God has been to you all of your life. "Oh, give thanks to the LORD, for *He is* good! For His mercy *endures* forever" (1 Chron. 16:34, NKJV).

There have been countless times in my life that I have taken time to meditate on God's goodness. In doing so, I remember the spiritual song sung by my mother, Calene Fowler, and my dad, Kinnie Fowler, as he played the song on his guitar. Some of the lyrics are:

"Count your blessings,

Name them one by one;

Count your many blessings and see what the Lord has done."

Our blessings outweigh those difficult days and times. Moreover, meditating about God's goodness puts a smile on the face of believers. Strength is renewed as you praise God and think about the many blessings in your lifetime.

God chose Moses to lead the Israelites out of Egypt. All was going well until they got to the Red Sea. Oh, but God's goodness. God parted the Red Sea so that His people would keep walking on dry land. Once the Israelites all got away from the water, God commanded it to return to its normal form.

Miriam, the sister of Moses and Aaron, started playing her tambourine, and she and the other Israelite women danced and sang. Although they had many difficult days in Egypt, it was time to praise God and thank Him for His goodness. They were remembering the promises of God as they left the past behind them and looked to the future.

Each morning, believers have the opportunity to praise God for all He has done and for all He is going to do. Looking back will only be a stumbling block that interferes with what God is going to do. Meditate on His goodness and praise Him for all His goodness toward you.

PRAYER

Dear Heavenly Father, I pray You will help each one reading this to remember God's blessings. I pray that each one will take time to reflect on Your goodness toward them. I pray You will unlock hidden memories of how You've guided them through difficult days. I pray for memories of how You have restored hope, faith, and trust in You. I pray for memories of healing, memories of the day You tore down walls of confusion and provided a clear path to victory. I pray You will give each reader calmness and appreciation during their times of meditating about Your goodness. I pray You will give them faith and consistency in reading Your Word. I ask for these blessings, in the mighty name of Jesus. Amen.

YOUR THOUGHTS AND PRAYER REQUEST

SPIRITUAL ARMOR

*Put on the whole armor of God that you may be able to stand
against the wiles of the devil.*

—Ephesians 6:11 (NKJV)

The apostle Paul wrote a letter to the Ephesians, telling them to be strong in the Lord and in the power of His might. He also told them that in order to be ready for spiritual warfare, they needed to be properly clothed and carry the appropriate weapons.

They needed to gird their waist with truth. In other words, they needed to be truthful believers. Be honest and sincere with others and in all you do in life. Reading the Word of God will be truth to your spirit. Jesus said, "And you shall know the truth, and the truth shall make you free" (John 8:32, NKJV).

They needed to put on the breastplate of righteousness to give them covering when attacked by thoughts and actions that go against right living. Being knowledgeable about God's Word will give guidance to understanding the importance of wearing a breastplate of righteousness. "And whatever we ask we receive from Him, because we keep His commandments and do those things that are pleasing in His sight" (1 John 3:22, NKJV).

They needed to shod their feet with the preparation of the Gospel. This means to prepare for hearing the good news about Jesus. Good news that is preached or taught gives peace to those who believe. Once believers know about this good news, they should share it with others as well as their testimony about how the Gospel gives peace. So have your feet wrapped with the Gospel. "Now may the Lord of peace himself give you peace at all times in every way. The Lord be with you all." (2 Thessalonians 3:16, NKJV).

They needed to put on the shield of faith, which is needed during trials and tribulations. The believer's faith is used as a shield against doubt and weak belief. When you need protection, hold up your shield of faith. Hold it up when fear and depression start to enter your mind. In a letter written to the early Christian churches, James said, "But let him ask in faith, with no doubting, for he who doubts is like a wave of the sea driven and tossed by the wind" (James 1:6, NKJV).

They needed to put on the helmet of salvation. Salvation is the greatest gift a believer can receive; it's what Jesus died on the cross for. "For God so loved the world, that he gave his only begotten Son, that whosoever believeth in him should not perish, but have everlasting life" (John 3:16, KJV). This helmet is needed to keep thoughts about the truth and the goodness of God. "For by grace you have been saved through faith, and that not of yourselves; *it is* the gift of God, not of works, lest anyone should boast" (Eph. 2:8–9, NKJV).

They also needed to put on the sword of the Spirit, which represents God's Word. When sharpened, consistent study of God's Word will give the believer strength and authority and stop the enemy's attacks. Prayer and Bible scriptures are a two-edged sword to overcome temptation. "For the word of God *is* living and powerful, and sharper than any two-edged sword, piercing even to the division of soul and spirit, and of joints and marrow, and is a discerner of the thoughts and intents of the heart" (Heb. 4:12, NKJV).

Jesus used the sword of the Spirit when the devil took Him up on a high mountain and showed Him all the kingdoms of the world and their glory. Then he told Jesus all would be His if He would worship him. Jesus said, "Away with you, Satan! For it is written, 'You shall worship the LORD your God, and Him only you shall serve'" (Matt. 4:10, NKJV).

Prayer

Thank you, Jesus, for providing each one reading today's message with spiritual armor. I pray You will guide and strengthen them to gird their waist with the truth and to keep on the breastplate of righteousness. I pray You will instruct them to wrap their feet with the preparation of the Gospel, to always carry the shield of faith, to keep on their heads the helmet of salvation, and to always use their sword of the Spirit when tempted. I pray these blessings, in the mighty name of Jesus. Amen.

YOUR THOUGHTS AND PRAYER REQUEST

_____

_____

_____

_____

_____

_____

_____

_____

_____

_____

_____

_____

_____

_____

_____

_____

ACTIVATING YOUR FAITH

But without faith it is impossible to please Him, for he who comes to God must believe that He is, and that He is a rewarder of those who diligently seek Him.

—Hebrews 11:6 (NKJV)

A person's faith is activated the moment they believe Jesus died on the cross for all, was buried three days, and rose from the grave. He kept His promise. Believers are to be as consistently diligent in their faith as Elisha was.

Elisha asked Elijah, "Please let a double portion of your spirit be upon me" (2 Kings 2:9, NKJV). Elijah answered, "You have asked a hard thing. *Nevertheless,* if you see me *when I am* taken from you, it shall be so for you; but if not, it shall not be *so*" (2 Kings 2:10, NKJV). Hearing these words, Elisha's faith was activated. He stayed with Elijah and saw him transported to heaven in a whirlwind. When Elijah dropped the anointed mantle, Elisha was right there to pick it up; he was consistent and determined.

For believers to please God, faith must be an active part of their character. We must believe God is who He says He is and that He will do what He says He will do. That's what knowing His character means.

Love is an essential part of God's character. "Oh, give thanks to God of Heaven! His mercy endures forever" (Psalm, NKJV).

Grace is God's kindness toward us; it is favor that we do not deserve, accompanied by His spiritual blessings. "For by grace you have been saved through faith, and that not of yourselves; *it is* the gift of God" (Eph. 2:8, NKJV).

In Matthew 9:35–36, Jesus showed compassion to a crowd of people who had followed Him, many of whom had traveled long distances to see Him. He healed the sick among them and fed the five thousand men, women, and children with only five loaves of bread and two fishes. The multitude ate until they were no longer hungry. Upon witnessing these miracles, the crowd's faith was activated.

In Daniel 3:16–26, three Hebrew boys, Shadrach, Meshach, and Abednego, activated their faith when they refused to bow down to a golden image. Their faith stayed activated even though King Nebuchadnezzar carried out his threat and put them into the fiery furnace. When Nebuchadnezzar looked into the furnace, he saw four men, and the fourth one looked like the Son of God. They were not hurt, for there was not a burn mark on them, and their clothes were not singed. Activating their faith kept the three Hebrew boys safe and protected.

Each time those who believe in Jesus trust Him, their faith is activated. As they learn to trust Jesus without doubting, their faith becomes stronger. Faith is also activated when a person hears and reads the Word of God. "Trust in the LORD with all your heart, And lean not on your own under-standing; In all your ways acknowledge Him, And He shall direct your paths" (Prov. 3:5–6, NKJV).

PRAYER

I'm asking everyone reading today's message to lift your hands to heaven and give God praise. Dear Heavenly Father, I thank You for all You have done in the life of each reader. I praise You for what You are going to do. I praise You for faith being activated as each person reads each line in today's message. I ask for this special blessing, in the mighty name of Jesus. Amen.

YOUR THOUGHTS AND PRAYER REQUEST

_____

_____

_____

_____

_____

_____

_____

_____

_____

_____

_____

_____

_____

_____

_____

JOSHUA AND CALEB

For we walk by faith, not by sight

—2 Corinthians 5:7 (NKJV)

Joshua and Caleb were the only two Israelites who demonstrated an activated faith. God had delivered the Israelites from being slaves in Egypt, took them through the Red Sea on dry land, and fed and clothed them the entire time they were in the wilderness.

Joshua and Caleb were chosen, with ten other Israelite men, to explore the Promised Land. After exploration, they reported to Moses and all the Israelites that the land flowed with milk and honey, and then they showed them the fruit. Their report generated doubt, however, because the people who lived in the Promised Land were powerful, and their cities were large and heavily protected. But Joshua and Caleb activated their faith by saying, "Let us go up at once and take possession, for we are well able to overcome it" (Num. 13:30, NKJV).

They also tried to activate the faith of Moses and all the Israelites by telling them that God would be with them. Due to their lack of faith, however, God made the Israelites wait forty years before they could enter the Promised Land. Every Israelite twenty years of age and older would die in the wilderness. This included Moses. But Caleb and Joshua saw the Promised

Land because they trusted God. What they saw with the natural eye didn't matter, because they saw the Promised Land with their spiritual eyesight.

My hope is that all who believe and have faith in God may be strengthened by Joshua and Caleb's spiritual eyesight. Hold strong to your faith no matter what you see with your natural eyes. Don't follow those who have no faith, and know that God will take you into all He has promised to do in your life.

PRAYER

Dear Heavenly Father, I praise You for what You are doing in the life of each one who has read today's message. There is no one like You, Jesus. I praise You for being reliable, powerful, and all-knowing. I pray for activated faith to rise up in the life of everyone reading today's message. I pray You will bless each one above their expectations. I pray for these blessings, in the mighty name of Jesus. Amen.

YOUR THOUGHTS AND PRAYER REQUEST

_____

_____

_____

_____

_____

_____

_____

_____

_____

_____

_____

_____

_____

_____

_____

_____

DAY 33

THIRST FOR GOD

As the deer pants for the water brooks, So pants my soul for You, O God.

—Psalm 42:1 (NKJV)

The deer's natural thirst is satisfied with water. After getting to streams of water, the deer's added safety occurs when stepping into water. Water blots out the deer's smell providing safety from enemies. Reading God's word provides safety for believers. When the deer arrives at the riverbank, it will not drink from the brook right away. After patiently waiting to make sure its environment is safe, the deer bows its head to drink from the brook. When a believer encounters trials and tribulations, bowing the head to pray is giving respect to God. Like the deer, waiting patiently and trusting God to lead and direct, gives self-assurance.

Believers pant for the righteousness of God and seek to live according to His will and His way, not of our own. "Blessed are those who hunger and thirst for righteousness, For they shall be filled" (Matt. 5:6, NKJV). Our thirst for God can't be satisfied by affection, employment, numerous followers on social media, or winning the lottery. Even if we managed to have all these things in life, there will still be a thirst.

Think about how blessed you are. Lift hands toward heaven and praise God for all His goodness toward you. Praise Him for strength, patience, and a desire to live a life that is pleasing in His sight. God knows your needs and He knows your name. Thirsting for the righteousness of God is sufficient. Always collaborate with God; tell Him all about your heart's desires.

I'm reminded of the lyrics to a song that we sang in church when I was a child. I hope these words will inspire you:

"Oh, when I think of the goodness of Jesus.
And all that He has done for me.
My soul cries out Hallelujah,
I thank God for saving me."

A believer's thirst for God is satisfied by hearing and reading His Word. Those who pant for spiritual nourishment and feast daily on the Word of God will be satisfied. Should believers forget or be caught up in the cares of this world, the Holy Spirit will assist in restoring their minds to thirsting for the righteousness of God. The apostle Paul tells us, "Do not be conformed to this world, but be transformed by the renewing of your mind, that you may prove what *is* that good and acceptable and perfect will of God" (Rom. 12:2, NKJV).

PRAYER

Dear Heavenly Father, I give You praise as I continue to pray for each one reading today's message. I pray You will increase faith and restore all that has been taken from those who believe in You. I pray for encouragement through Your Word and through prayer. I pray for those who thirst to seek after You, like the deer pants for the water brook. I pray You will satisfy their thirst with righteousness, with discernment, and with patience. I pray for these blessings, in the mighty name of Jesus. Amen.

"You shall love the LORD your God with all your heart, with all your soul, and with all your mind" (Matt. 22:37, NKJV).

YOUR THOUGHTS AND PRAYER REQUEST

SELF-CARE

A HEALTH-CONSCIOUS LIFE

Or do you not know that your body is the temple of the Holy Spirit who is in you, whom you have from God, and you are not your own? For you were bought at a price; therefore glorify God in your body and in your spirit, which are God's.

—1 Corinthians 6:19–20 (NKJV)

After the birth of my oldest grandson, Elijah, I started thinking about my health with curiosity. In doing so, researching and food planning became more important than they had been in the past. Why? Because I wanted to be a grandmother who would be a blessing in Elijah's life for a long time. My prayer for wisdom has included putting an emphasis on good health and long life.

Seventeen years later, God blessed me with my youngest grandchild. Her name is Melina. My prayer, linked with research about nutritious eating, has become more powerful in my daily life than ever before. Asking God for long life and good health requires faith and works.

There were foods from my childhood I had to let go of, as well as cooking methods that were destroying my temple of the Holy Spirit. Research helped me realize that quick meals from the drive-through were not healthy and would contribute to diseases in the body.

My hope is that today's message will be welcomed by all who are reading. I also want to provide awareness about foods that will supply the body with nutrients. Everyone makes choices about what they put into their temples. I want to encourage prayer for guidance and for spiritual insight into how to prepare meals that will provide the best nutrients. Also, if possible, stay away from those foods that do not contain nutrients.

Having been a member of Kaiser Permanente, I had the opportunity to attend a twelve-week program titled, "RENEW Program: A Program to Explore Healthy Possibilities." I learned to minimize processed foods, including sugar, white flour, and oil, and eat a big green salad. I also learned you can add items to salads or other foods, such as berries, onions, garlic, ginger, turmeric, cinnamon, paprika, rosemary, oregano, thyme, and mushrooms. The program also recommended eating beans and lentils. Choosing to eat healthy may eliminate paying for weight-control supplements or foods. Eating foods filled with micronutrients may be the path for a health-conscious life.

I hope my testimony will encourage others to seek guidance for better health. Moreover, linking prayer, faith, understanding, and a little work (planning and preparing healthy snacks and meals each day) may be beneficial toward acquiring the best health.

PRAYER

Thank you, Jesus, so much for this opportunity to do good things for others. I pray You move powerfully in the lives of all who want to live healthier. I pray that what may seem impossible will become possible. I pray You will tear down walls that are blocking the path to better health. I pray You give each reader a desire to look to their future and to let go of past failures, past disappointments, past regrets, and past hurts. I pray You will move each one into the arena of faith with works, believing and not doubting. I pray for spiritual eyesight, strength, and endurance. I ask for these blessings, in the mighty name of Jesus. Amen.

YOUR THOUGHTS AND PRAYER REQUEST

_____

_____

_____

_____

_____

_____

_____

_____

_____

_____

_____

_____

_____

_____

_____

Journey Toward Optimal Health

For with God nothing will be impossible.

—Luke 1:37 (NKJV)

This journey is a choice. Choosing a journey toward optimal health is to be healthy throughout life. My desire is to help my adult children and my grandchildren live a healthy lifestyle. In doing so, I needed to make changes to my lifestyle, including planning healthy meals and doing simple exercises. Experience has taught me to choose exercises that would allow for sustainability. Here are some easy exercises I believe will assist with sustainable routines at home:

Easy Sitting Exercise:

a. Sit comfortably in a sturdy chair that will allow you to raise and lower your arms.
b. Relax both arms with hands on your knees.
c. Slowly raise both arms into the air.
d. Hold for five seconds and start to slowly lower both arms.

Repeat this exercise for five rounds.

Relax.

Add deep breathing to this exercise:

a. When slowly raising your arms, breathe deeply in through your nose.
b. When lowering your arms, breathe out through your mouth, looking straight in front of you and imagining you're blowing out a candle.

Repeat this exercise for five rounds.

Relax.

Easy Standing Exercise:

a. Stand next to a sturdy chair.
b. Put one hand on the top back of the sturdy chair and hold tightly.
c. Raise yourself up on the balls of your feet and lower back down.

Repeat ten times.

Relax.

After this exercise, do deep breathing:

a. Deeply breathe in through your nose.
b. Breathe out through your mouth. Imagine you're blowing out a candle.

Repeat five times.

I recommend doing these exercises at least two times a day, once before noon and once before 7:00 p.m. Over time you will notice increased endurance, focus, strength, and sustainability.

The importance of breathing exercises during your journey toward optimal health is emphasized by Dr. James Hoyt: "Though it may feel unnatural to breathe deeply, the practice comes with various benefits. Deep breaths are more efficient: they allow your body to fully exchange incoming oxygen with outgoing carbon dioxide. They have also been shown to slow the heartbeat, lower or stabilize blood pressure, and lower stress."

The Bible gives an account of Job's journey. After all he suffered, he reclaimed his mental and physical health. His wife told him to curse God and die, and his friends visited him with negative advice, which Job would not accept. But as long as he could breathe, Job knew that God would deliver him. He said, "As long as my breath is in me, And the breath of God in my nostrils" (Job 27:3, NKJV). As long as God gives you the blessing of breathing, you can make healthy choices.

Please consult your doctor before doing any of the recommended physical or breathing exercises.

Prayer

Dear Heavenly Father, I praise You for Your kindness and tender mercy as those who believe and trust in You step forward on a journey toward ultimate health. I pray You will guide each one to the right food choices and increase their understanding as never before. I ask that You give wisdom, patience, endurance, and determination. I pray that each bit of food will send nourishment to the blood cells, to the heart, to the kidneys, to the liver, and to the lungs, as well as blot out every disease, now and in the future. I pray for restored health and strength. I ask for these blessings, in the mighty name of Jesus. Amen.

YOUR THOUGHTS AND PRAYER REQUEST

Benefits of Walking

Beloved, I pray that you may prosper in all things and be in health, just as your soul prospers.

—3 John 1:2 (NKJV)

Walking is simply moving by lifting each foot and putting it down, alternately. In doing some research for this chapter, I realized that many doctors recommend walking. Dr. Paul Oh says, "It's a simple and accessible all-purpose activity."

Walking increases cardiovascular and pulmonary as well as heart and lung fitness, and it reduces the risks of heart disease or a stroke. It also improves conditions such as hypertension, high blood pressure, high cholesterol, joint and muscular pain or stiffness, and diabetes. In addition, it aids in producing stronger bones and improved balance.

According to Larry Kidder, of Loma Linda University, "The benefits of consistent walking are almost at the same levels as aerobic exercise in regards to general health—and cardiovascular health in particular. In addition, the damage of joints caused by many forms of strenuous aerobic exercise is often conveniently overlooked."

The Mayo Clinic reports, "Walking in place is just as effective as walking on a track; all you need is enough space to march, supportive shoes, and comfortable clothing. The key to weight loss while walking is raising your heart rate 50 to 70 percent of your maximum heart rate, exercising at a moderately intense speed."

Before starting an in-home walking exercise program, get a pair of good shoes designed for walking. They should be comfortable and supportive but not snug or constricting.

Simple walking exercise in your home:

1. Choose a spacious area in the home.
2. Warm up by casually walking from one end of a room to the other (Repeat five times).
3. Start walking in place.
4. Raise your arms up and down as you're walking.
5. Depending on your endurance level, count to 100 and stop.

Relax.

After relaxing and still standing, do some deep-breathing exercises:

a. Breathe in through the nose.
b. Breathe out through the mouth. Imagine you're blowing out a candle. (Repeat five times).

Relax.

If possible, do this simple walking exercise at least twice a day: once before noon, and once in the afternoon, before 7:00 p.m.

Please consult your doctor before doing these exercises.

PRAYER

Dear Heavenly Father, I give You praise, and I thank You for Your guidance, wisdom, knowledge, and understanding. I pray that each one reading today's message will become healthier and stay healthy. I pray You give them strength with every breath they take. These blessings, I ask for, in the matchless name of Jesus. Amen.

YOUR THOUGHTS AND PRAYER REQUEST

Food Choices

A s born-again believers, we feed our souls with the Word of God. In doing so, we strive for a more filling spiritual life, knowing that prayer gives power and strength. When we listen to God's preached or taught Word, the Holy Spirit guides us away from those who speak falsely. In comparison, when reading a menu, wisdom and knowledge about foods will lead believers to make the best choices. This chapter looks at foods that will benefit the heart and those that won't.

The heart distributes blood, oxygen, and nutrients throughout the body. To function as God intended, it needs to be healthy. The following foods and spices presented on WebMD will give you the guidance you need to be heart-healthy.

Sugar, salt, and fat have high amounts of saturated fat and refined carbs that will raise your risk for a heart attack or stroke.

Bacon contains approximately 50 percent saturated fat, which can raise bad cholesterol and increase chances of having a heart attack or stroke. There is a lot of salt in bacon that raises the blood pressure and causes the heart to work harder.

Too much red meat—beef, lamb, and pork—may lead to a higher risk of heart disease and diabetes, most likely, because these meats are high in saturated fat, which can raise cholesterol. Consider lowering the portions of red meat you take in. If your diet must contain red meats, consider lean cuts like round sirloin and extra lean ground beef.

A can of soda has more added sugar than is recommended for a whole day. Soda drinkers tend to gain more weight and are more likely to become obese and have type 2 diabetes, high blood pressure, and heart disease. It is best to drink plain water, carbonated water, or unsweetened flavored water.

Cookies, cakes, and muffins should be rare treats. They're typically loaded with added sugar, which leads to weight gain. These goodies are linked to higher triglyceride levels that can lead to heart disease. Usually, the main ingredients are white flour, which may spike your blood sugar and increase hunger. To make healthier treats, bake with whole-wheat flour, trim the sugar, and use liquid plant oils instead of butter or shortening.

Processed meats like hot dogs, sausage, salami, and lunch meats are the worst types of meats for the heart. They have high amounts of salt, and most are high in saturated fat. When comparing deli meats, turkey is best, but it does contain sodium even though it doesn't have the saturated fat content. Turkey deli meat is not as heart-healthy as a fresh sliced turkey breast.

Think before choosing to eat white rice, bread, and pasta. Healthy fiber, vitamins, and minerals are missing from foods made with white flour. Refined grains will quickly convert to sugar, which the body stores as fat. A diet high in refined grains can cause belly fat, which is linked to heart disease and type 2 diabetes. It is best to get at least half your grains from whole grains like brown rice, oats, and whole wheat. When shopping, look for the words "100 percent whole grain."

Pizza is a quick and easy meal, but most take-out pizzas and frozen pies have staggering amounts of sodium, fat, and calories, all of which can raise the risk of a heart attack. Best choice for pizza is thin crust, and, if possible, whole wheat. Request less cheese on pizza and more vegetables. Leave off pepperoni and sausage; they're filled with salt. Pizza can be healthier when personally made.

Drinking alcohol moderately won't harm the heart, unless your health records show high blood pressure or high triglycerides, a type of fat (lipid) found in the blood. The body converts any calories it doesn't need to use right away into triglycerides, which are then stored in fat cells. Later, hormones release triglycerides for energy between meals.

Heavy drinking, on the other hand, can lead to high blood pressure, heart failure, strokes, and weight gain. If you don't already drink, it would be best not to start.

Butter is high in saturated fat, which can raise bad cholesterol and make heart disease more likely. It may be better to replace butter with olive oil or vegetable oil-based spreads, which contain heart-healthy mono- and polyunsaturated fats. If high cholesterol is present in the body, use stanol as a spread. Regular use of stanol can lower low-density lipoprotein (LDL).

Yogurt can be a super source of nutrition. Eating it regularly might protect you from high blood pressure. It's important to be aware of the different kinds of yogurt, when buying. Flavored yogurts are full of added sugar, which is linked to weight gain, high blood pressure, inflammation, and heart disease. The healthy choice is plain low-fat yogurt. Fresh fruit, cinnamon, or vanilla can be added for taste and flavor.

French fries are a must for many, but eating deep-fried potatoes from restaurants and fast-food places contain lots of fat and salt, which is bad news for the heart. It is healthier to eat a small portion, or, even better, make oven-baked fries with heart-healthy olive oil. Even better, use sweet potatoes.

Fried chicken or deep-fried chicken adds calories, fat, and sodium to an otherwise-healthy food. Studies have linked fried foods to the development of type 2 diabetes, obesity, and high blood pressure, all of which raise the odds of heart failure. For a crispy, but healthier choice, bread chicken breasts in whole-wheat flour and bake instead of frying.

Canned soup can be an easy way to get more vegetables, protein, and fiber, but be sure to look for unhealthy ingredients. Canned soup often has lots of sodium that can cause high blood pressure, heart attack, stroke, and heart failure. Cream-based soups have unhealthy saturated fat. The healthiest way to enjoy soup is to make it from scratch with a low-sodium broth. If buying prepared soup, check the label for the least amount of salt and fat.

Ranch dressing's main ingredients are buttermilk, salt, and sugar. This makes it high in fat, sodium, and calories, none of which is good for the heart. To make a healthy version of this creamy dressing, blend low-fat sour cream or cottage cheese with low-fat buttermilk and fresh herbs like dill, tarragon, or chives.

Ice cream is high in sugar, calories, and saturated fat. So, save it for a special treat. Eating foods loaded with fat and sugar leads to weight gain. It can also drive up triglycerides and lead to a heart attack. Cut calories and fat by choosing sorbet, low-fat or nonfat frozen yogurt, or frozen fruit bars. Check the label for the least amount of sugar and saturated fat.

Potato chips are one of the foods that contribute most to weight gain. Not only are they loaded with saturated fat but they're covered in salt, which is also linked to heart disease. Skip the lower-sodium or low-fat potato chips. They'll just leave you hungry again. The most nutritious snacks have a combination of healthy proteins, carbs, and fats, like whole-grain crackers with low-fat cheese or homemade popcorn, tossed with olive oil.

I pray that you will take time to ponder all of this information, to be truly blessed, when making healthy food choices.

PRAYER

Dear Heavenly Father, I humbly come before You, lifting my hands in praise. Your grace is sufficient in the life of all who believe and trust in You. Your guidance is a blessing, and Your love is forever. Thank You for teaching each one who has been reading today's message more about living and growing a more prosperous and healthier life. Thank You for opening spiritual eyes so believers will see Your love. I pray for strength, understanding, and endurance for each one. I believe there is going to be a change in the life of each believer. I pray You will give patience and unwavering trust day by day. These blessings I ask, in the name of Jesus. Amen.

YOUR THOUGHTS AND PRAYER REQUEST

Grow Your Garden

But grow in the grace and knowledge of our Lord and Savior Jesus Christ.

—2 Peter 3:18 (NKJV)

Each day those who trust and believe in God have an opportunity to grow a spiritual flower garden. To start growing your garden, follow these essential steps.

Plant seeds of faith; in fact, saturate the ground with faith so that your flowers will grow healthy and bring about life-changing results.

Mix with your faith with seeds of positive thinking. Healthy thinking is needed for your future success.

Pull up from your garden all negativity. These are the weeds (the words of negative-speaking people) that will grow around your faith and choke it out.

Plant seeds of a positive attitude so that beautiful flowers will grow and bring positive-speaking people into your life.

Plant seeds of expectation. These seeds will grow into flowers that will bloom throughout your day. Expect God to work in every area of your life.

Planting seeds of gratefulness will grow flowers that will gracefully bow with thanksgiving in every pedal. Thank God for all He has done, is doing, and will be doing in your life.

Plant seeds of confidence in your garden to raise your self-esteem, your confidence, as well as your belief and trust in God. You will see yourself making good decisions throughout your walk with Jesus.

Seeds of kindness are a must have for all believers. Your flower will be radiantly bright and have a sweet fragrance, which will manifest in giving kind words to others, and sharing with those in need, as your flower grows. God will bless you and you will be a blessing.

Always water your garden with the words of God. As your garden grows, you will be nourished with wisdom, knowledge, and understanding in all areas of your life.

I want to encourage all believers to grow in the grace of God. This growth may not take place overnight. Just be patient and remain strong in your faith, day by day. On those days when your garden starts showing weeds, don't hesitate to pull up every one of them from the root. Put a stop to negative people and conversations.

Prayer

Dear Heavenly Father, I pray for those who are reading today's message to grow in their spiritual walks with You. I pray You will teach each reader how to speak blessings into the lives of others so they may grow in the grace and knowledge of You. I pray for deliverance from all that might hinder those who desire to grow spiritually. These blessings I ask, in the mighty name of Jesus. Amen.

WRITE DOWN YOUR BLESSINGS
SEE ALL THAT GOD HAS DONE FOR YOU

REFERENCES

(Day 8)

"When you feed on Jesus, the most well-loved psalm in the Bible, Psalm 23, paints a beautiful picture of our good shepherd, Jesus, caring for His loved flock. He feeds, protects, and leads us to rest so that we lack no good thing. You can experience the abundant life that Jesus has for you when you allow Him to shepherd and feed you. When you focus on Him and feed on His love for you and His living words, you will find rest for your souls, victory over the most trying circumstances, and an abundance of every good thing! The abundant life refers to life in its abounding fullness of joy and strength for spirit, soul, and body."

Citation:

"Hear Your Way to the Abundant Life: Joseph Prince Ministries", accessed, October 17, 2014.
https://www.josephprince.org

(Day 15)

Forgiveness doesn't mean forgetting or excusing the harm done to you or making up with the person who caused the harm. Forgiveness brings a kind of peace that helps you go on with life.

Citation:

"Forgiveness: Letting go of grudges and bitterness: Mayo Clinic Staff", accessed July 8, 2021.
mcl@mayo.edu (United Stated)
mliintl@mayo.edu (International)

(Day 15)

There is no instant cure for jealousy. But accepting that jealousy is normal, challenging negative thoughts, and practicing mindfulness may all help reduce its pull."

Citation:

"Jealousy: Psychology Today", accessed March 10, 2020.
https//www.psychologytoday.com/us/basics/jealousy
psychologytoday.com

(Day 15)

"It can be excruciatingly difficult to deal with negative people—people who bring your mood down with their pessimism, anxiety, and general sense of distrust."

Citation:

"Psychology Today: Dealing with Negative People", accessed March 3, 2021. https://www.psychologytoday.com psychologytoday.com

(Page 23)

Webster's Dictionary defines being steadfast as being "Firmly fixed in place" or "Firm in belief, determination." The Lord did not say that believing and trusting in Him would mean a life of prosperity and no hardships or struggles.

Citation:

"About Webster Dictionary: Webster Dictionary", accessed, March 16, 2021, https://www.merriam-webster.com > steadfast-2017-07-17

(Day 26)

The American Psychological Association says, "Anxiety is an emotion characterized by feelings of tension, worried thoughts and physical changes, like increased blood pressure." Furthermore, "People with anxiety disorders usually have recurring intrusive thoughts or concerns. They may also avoid certain situations because of worry and may have physical symptoms such as sweating, trembling, dizziness, or a rapid heartbeat."

Citation:

"About The American Psychology Association: The American Psychology Association", accessed, March 23, 2021.
Home//Psychology Topics//Anxiety

(Day 28)

Anxiety is an emotion characterized by feelings of tension, worried thoughts and physical changes like increased blood pressure.
People with anxiety disorders usually have recurring intrusive thoughts or concerns. They may avoid certain situations due to worry. Also, they may also have physical symptoms such as swearing, trembling, dizziness or a rapid heartbeat.

Citation:

American Psychological Association, "Anxiety:
https://www.apa.org/topics/anxiety

(Day 34)

Having been a member of Kaiser Permanente, I had the opportunity to attend a twelve-week program titled, "RENEW Program: A Program to Explore Healthy Possibilities."

Citation

Fuhrman, Joel, M.D. "Eating to Live" Renew A Lifestyle Approach to Diabetes: Kaiser Permanente, August 16, 2017.

(Day 35)

The importance of breathing exercises during your journey toward optimal health is emphasized by Dr. James Hoyt: "Though it may feel unnatural to breathe deeply, the practice comes with various benefits. Deep breaths are more efficient: they allow your body to fully exchange incoming oxygen with outgoing carbon dioxide. They have also been shown to slow the heartbeat, lower or stabilize blood pressure, and lower stress."

Citation

"Understanding breathing and the importance of taking a deep breath: UC Health Today", accessed April 4, 2021. https://www.uchealth.org/contact-us/

(Day 36)

Walking is simply moving by lifting each foot and putting it down, alternately. In doing some research for this chapter, I realized that many doctors recommend walking. Dr. Paul Oh says, "It's a simple and accessible all-purpose activity."

Citation

"Indoors or out it's time to get walking: Health Advisor", accessed November 27, 2020. https://www.theglobeandmail.com

(Day 36)

According to Larry Kidder of Loma Linda University, "The benefits of consistent walking are almost at the same levels as aerobic exercise in regards to general health—and cardiovascular health in particular. In addition, the damage of joints caused by many forms of strenuous aerobic exercise is often conveniently overlooked."

Citation

"Loma Linda University Dyson Center: Condition your Muscles and Burn More Calories, access August 15, 2019. https://drayson.llu.edu/about/contact-us

(Day 36)

The Mayo Clinic reports, "Walking in place is just as effective as walking on a track; all you need is enough space to march, supportive shoes, and comfortable clothing. The key to weight loss while walking is raising your heart rate 50 to 70 percent of your maximum heart rate, exercising at a moderately intense speed."

<u>Citation</u>

"Walking in place is just as effective as walking on a track: Mayo Clinic", accessed, May 3, 2021
https//www.mayoclinic.org
"About The American Psychology Association: The American Psychology Association", accessed, March 23, 2021.
Home//Psychology Topics//Anxiety

(Day 37)

The heart distributes blood, oxygen, and nutrients throughout the body. To function as God intended, it needs to be healthy. The following foods and spices presented in WebMD will give you the guidance you need to be heart-healthy.

Public Domains are:

(Day 29)

There is no Citation, because church members put words together, over 60 years ago.
"Count your blessings,
Name them one by one;
Count your many blessings and see what the Lord has done."

(Day 33)

<u>There is no Citation, because church</u> members put words together, over 60 years ago.

"Oh, when I think of the goodness of Jesus.

And all that He has done for me.

My soul cries out Hallelujah,

I thank God for saving me."

CPSIA information can be obtained
at www.ICGtesting.com
Printed in the USA
BVHW062109020122
625336BV00005B/106